Storytelling

SERIES EDITORS

David E. Johnson *Comparative Literature, University at Buffalo*
Scott Michaelsen *English, Michigan State University*

SERIES ADVISORY BOARD

Nahum D. Chandler, *African American Studies, University of California, Irvine*
Rebecca Comay, *Philosophy and Comparative Literature, University of Toronto*
Marc Crépon, *Philosophy, École Normale Supérieure, Paris*
Jonathan Culler, *Comparative Literature, Cornell University*
Johanna Drucker, *Design Media Arts and Information Studies,
University of California, Los Angeles*
Christopher Fynsk, *Modern Thought, Aberdeen University*
Rodolphe Gasché, *Comparative Literature, University at Buffalo*
Martin Hägglund, *Comparative Literature, Yale University*
Carol Jacobs, *German and Comparative Literature, Yale University*
Peggy Kamuf, *French and Comparative Literature, University of Southern California*
David Marriott, *History of Consciousness, University of California, Santa Cruz*
Steven Miller, *English, University at Buffalo*
Alberto Moreiras, *Hispanic Studies, Texas A&M University*
Patrick O'Donnell, *English, Michigan State University*
Pablo Oyarzún, *Teoría del Arte, Universidad de Chile*
Scott Cutler Shershow, *English, University of California, Davis*
Henry Sussman, *German and Comparative Literature, Yale University*
Samuel Weber, *Comparative Literature, Northwestern University*
Ewa Ziarek, *Comparative Literature, University at Buffalo*

Storytelling

The Destruction of the Inalienable in
the Age of the Holocaust

Rodolphe Gasché

Cover: Helen Frankenthaler, "Holocaust." © 2018 Helen Frankenthaler Foundation, Inc. / Artists Rights Society (ARS), New York.

Published by State University of New York Press, Albany

© 2018 State University of New York

All rights reserved

No part of this book may be used or reproduced in any manner whatsoever without written permission. No part of this book may be stored in a retrieval system or transmitted in any form or by any means including electronic, electrostatic, magnetic tape, mechanical, photocopying, recording, or otherwise without the prior permission in writing of the publisher.

For information, contact State University of New York Press, Albany, NY
www.sunypress.edu

Library of Congress Cataloging-in-Publication Data

Names: Gasché, Rodolphe, author.
Title: Storytelling : the destruction of the inalienable in the age of the
    Holocaust / Rodolphe Gasché
Description: Albany : State University of New York, [2018] | Series: SUNY
    series, literature in theory | Includes bibliographical references and
    index.
Identifiers: LCCN 2017054958| ISBN 9781438471457 (hardcover
    : alk. paper) | 9781438471464 (pbk. : alk. paper) | ISBN
    9781438471471 (e-book)
Subjects: LCSH: Storytelling--Philosophy. | Storytelling in literature. |
    Holocaust, Jewish (1939-1945)—Influence. | Schapp, Wilhelm, 1884-1965. |
    Benjamin, Walter, 1892-1940. | Arendt, Hannah, 1906-1975.
Classification: LCC PN56.S7357 G37 2018 | DDC 809/.93353—dc23
LC record available at https://lccn.loc.gov/2017054958

10 9 8 7 6 5 4 3 2 1

For Bronia Karst

CONTENTS

	Acknowledgments	ix
PRELIMINARIES	On Not Telling Stories	1
CHAPTER 1	Entanglement in Stories (Wilhelm Schapp)	41
CHAPTER 2	Storytelling (Walter Benjamin)	57
CHAPTER 3	Surviving for Others (Hannah Arendt)	81
POSTLIMINARIES	Storytelling and World Loss	111
	Notes	123
	Index	149

ACKNOWLEDGMENTS

THE PARTS OF THIS ESSAY THAT ARE DEVOTED TO THE NARRAtive theories, more precisely to the theories of storytelling by Wilhelm Schapp, Walter Benjamin, and Hannah Arendt, were first presented on the invitation of Gerhard Richter on the occasion of a three-day seminar in October 2016 at Brown University. The section on Wilhelm Schapp was the material for a seminar that I held the same year at the University of Tokyo on the invitation of Hiroki Yoshikuni. Finally the part of Benjamin became the basis for a workshop that at the invitation of María del Rosario Acosta López I directed at DePaul University in the spring of 2017. In short, I am delighted to acknowledge a wide array of debts. I owe deep thanks to Gerhard Richter, Hiroki Yoshikuni, and María del Rosario Acosta López not only for having given me an opportunity to test the ideas presented in this essay, but also for the valuable questions and suggestions they offered. My thanks also go to Bonnie Honig, Thomas Schestag, Susan Bernstein, Kristina Mendicino at Brown University; to Yusuke Myazaki, and Kai Gohara at Tokyo; and finally to Peg Birmingham, Elizabeth Millan, Elizabeth Rottenberg, and in particular María del Rosario Acosta at DePaul University, whose timely and insightful comments and questions shaped the final version of this work.

Finally, I am grateful to Nicole Sweeney Allen who assisted me in the preparation of the manuscript.

PRELIMINARIES

On Not Telling Stories

FROM EARLY ON PHILOSOPHY HAS IMPOSED ON ITSELF THE exigency not to tell stories (*mython tina diegesthai*). However, this injunction is not a hostile repudiation by an already constituted genre of discourse other than storytelling. On the contrary, the demand is the constituting gesture of philosophical logos which consists, prior to all its more specific concerns, of nothing other than this withdrawal or stepping back from storytelling, which clears a place for posing questions, above all regarding storytelling—that is, the narrative form in which the question of Being found its first formulation. Indeed, as posed in the story told by Parmenides, the question of the *on* could be raised only in such a story as something purely abstract, and in negation of all particularities. Even though philosophy may, perhaps, never have gone one step further than its inaugural gesture of keeping alive the question concerning Being that arose in the stories told about it by the pre-Socratic philosophers—everything else in philosophy remaining, then, of the order of storytelling—philosophy, when true to its founding gesture, consists in not telling stories. As the Stranger in Plato's *Sophist* remarks, one cannot proceed in a narrative way especially when Being itself is at issue.[1] Telling stories about Being is to speak about it in inadequate, metaphorical—that is, in ontic terms—that miss Being itself. Even though philosophy has not always lived up to this uncompromising demand inherent in it, philosophy from Plato to Husserl and Heidegger is predicated on this interdiction of telling stories. But even in Plato this relation between philosophy and storytelling is considerably more complex. The philosophical *logos* does not simply exclude mythos from itself—at times a recourse to myth becomes inevitable, especially, as in the case of *The Statesman*, when, according to Plato's words, the argument—*logos*—needs to be rescued from disgrace.[2] As a consequence, philosophy has always kept intact its ability to tell stories, even to the point of considering a return in early German Romanticism to what, then, was called *erzählende Philosophie* (narrativizing philosophy). But what if this ability to tell stories has itself become, not simply endangered, but radically impaired? Or if such an inability is caused by something that no longer lets itself be told and that defies the intelligibility that the form of a story could impart on it? Is an inability to tell stories something that philosophy ought to worry about? After all, its interdiction to tell stories presupposes as such the possibility of narrating stories; it assumes that telling stories is indeed an intrinsic part of the natural attitude to be overcome when certain questions are to be adequately posed and addressed. But if it becomes impossible to tell stories, and philosophy cannot revert to them in case of need, philosophy's interdiction of telling stories becomes problematic. How can philosophy insist on prohibiting what it once considered the most natural ability of the human being, storytelling, if it may no longer even be possible to perform? Furthermore, if philosophy should have to confront the question of being unable to proceed in a narrative way regarding certain phenomena, how should it proceed? Would it not require philosophy to inquire anew into the nature of stories and to recast itself and its exigencies in the face of the untellable, and eventually in the face of the muteness of the one who is expected to have the inalienable mental power to speak about it in the form of stories?

❖ ❖ ❖

According to Plato's dialogue, philosophy wishes to mute *muthoi* within its *logoi*, or rather, in the *logos* about Being. But perhaps philosophy is less concerned with another type of tale or story, the *ainos*. However, in Plato's *Republic*, where one could imagine the *ainos* having a place for practical reasons, Plato speaks only of the fables and stories that are to be excluded from the city as *mythoi*. It is true that even though *ainos* is translated as "tale," or "fable," it is perhaps not a narrative genre all by itself. Rather, it may be considered merely a feature of stories, that like the oldest fables regarding animal figures in Greek literature, in particular those of Archilochus or Aesop, aim at exerting some form of social criticism. The story in Homer's *Odyssey* that the beggar Odysseus, in need of a cloak for the night, tells Eumaeus, who immediately understands the message and secures him covering for the cold night, demonstrates that the "archaic *ainos* is to be determined as a story that has been invented for a singular occasion, and whose purpose is to express in a veiled way that which, expressed directly, would be less effective and even harmful."[3] *Ainos* also designates a riddle.[4] Indeed, the ambivalent or enigmatic wording of its message requires decoding by the selected listener for whom its moral lesson is intended.

Yet what if stories are blocked from reaching out to others? What if the events that they narrate are such that they have divested their stories of all enigma or that, on the contrary, they are so enigmatic that they cannot be decoded anymore and thus cannot be made to work for an attentive listener? In both cases, the stories in question would have lost their power to convey a message, a moral, or a meaning. Are these stories, then, something that philosophy would not have to exclude from its discourse, neither for theoretical, nor for practical reasons, since the stories have already censured themselves? But what then of these stories that have altogether withdrawn from the practical realm and no longer need to be expelled? Does philosophical thought, in its practical application, not become affected by this inner muteness of certain stories?

❖ ❖ ❖

Muteness is not the same as being silent. According to Martin Heidegger, "[o]nly what can speak can be silent."⁵ To be silent presupposes the possibility of utterance since it consists only in refraining from speech. Silence, thus, is possible only where speaking is an option, where language as a whole is intact. Therefore, silence can give way to language; it is a condition from which language can arise. But silence is also the condition of possibility of who possess the capability to speak of being able to listen. But with muteness, though, we face an entirely different phenomenon. To be mute does not simply mean to be silent. The word "mute" (like its French equivalent "muet") comes from the Latin "mutus," which names the lack of possession of the faculty of speech and, by extension, the capability of producing only inarticulate sounds. The corresponding term in German, "stumm," originates in "stu" which derives from "stemmen" in Middle High German, whose original meaning is "impeding," "inhibiting," and "hampering," and indicates the lack of ability to emit lingual sounds. Muteness, where it is not a condition owed to a speech disorder or hearing loss, arises when language has been crippled and when the human being has been violently deprived of what, so far, has been the property that distinguishes it from animals. Unlike silence, muteness implies the impossibility of speech. From it no language can arise and one would have to ask what—for the one who has thus been deprived of speech—listening could still mean. Having been caused by violence, muteness is that from whence violence begins. Only events that are unutterable because language, understood as that which makes humans humans, has been destroyed, usher in muteness.

Besides the fact that language is meant for something other than rendering the unsayable, the crippling of language that causes muteness is not only the result of an act of violence, with the absence of words to speak about what has caused such muteness, it is both a state of extreme distress and one where violence starts. Again, being mute implies that the words, which would make it possible to speak, are missing. Muteness is caused by an abyssal distress that originates in the impossibility of providing the untellable with a crypt—"a kind of home that [it] may haunt at will," to quote Ruth Klüger—deferring the moment, perhaps forever, at which the untellable can be made intelligible.[6] But, at the same time, the inability to speak about the violent events that have caused the distress in question becomes a traumatic burden inflicted on those who *need* to know about what the muted person has undergone. The muteness inflicted on the victims by unspeakable events, in this way, is therefore not free from a certain violence.

But even though muteness consists in an inability to find words to communicate the events that has caused it, at the same time it is an appeal (however desperate), without words, for a word by others. "In the hollow of my muteness / lay a word," Ingeborg Bachmann writes in "Psalm."[7] The muted individual, rather than aurally detached, not only begs to be listened to, but also to be allowed to listen. Indeed, however paradoxical it may seem, if muteness as a hollow (*Mulde*) begs for a word, it is for it to be able to hear again. But the demand addressed to the other to form "a word" to be deposited in the hollow is, of course, also the demand for the mouth to be allowed to become a mouth again, however mute. Bachmann adds: "[A]nd grow tall forests on both sides, such that my mouth lies wholly in shade."[8] Only "a word," one word, is requested to be let to lie in its hollow in order for it to "say" its inability to tell while at the same time according it a retreat, the shelter in muteness. Lending the muted lips a word is in no way meant to saturate the receptacle of the voiceless lips by speaking loudly for it, or by usurping its name. All that the hollow of muteness requests is to lend it a word so that, affirmed, its muteness can speak to others while at the same time avoiding violence.

✦ ✦ ✦

"To speak" can mean very different things that are not to be conflated, such as providing information, giving testimony, or telling the story of what the survivors of unspeakable horror underwent. Providing information takes place in light of archival and historical work, while testifying to what happened during such events takes place in view of establishing in the capacity of a third (impartial observer) the facts for a trial, hence, for judging the events from a legal perspective.[9] In this essay, I am not concerned with the "story" of such an event itself, an event of which it is impossible to make sense by way of an account that has the form of a story, but only with this event's survivors and their refusal, or rather inability to tell their stories. In short, I am concerned with their muteness. This concurrence of an event that is not understandable and that strikes its survivors with muteness is certainly not accidental. Needless to say, I am referring to the holocaust.

No doubt, some will frown at the distinctions I make between modes of speech. They may see them as merely conceptual subtleties, especially in face of this admittedly monstrous event. However, the very emphasis that, depending on the context, the writings of the survivors put on one or the other of these activities shows that they are not designations of one and the same activity, despite the fact that the three linguistic activities are not always clearly distinguished in these writings or in the literature on the holocaust. The frequent observations regarding the victims' inability *to tell their stories* is another clear indication of the fact that their muteness is not the same as the inability to testify.

Life in the death camps has been regularly described by their survivors as one of sheer senselessness. Everything appeared orchestrated so as to prevent all predictability. Perhaps the guard's remark to Primo Levi's question of why he had brutally snatched away an icicle that, driven by thirst, Levi had broken off from the roof of the barrack—namely that "'*Hier is kein Warum*' (there is no why here)"—best describes the impossibility of making sense of what happened in the camps.[10] One could cite numerous references to this experience of systematic arbitrariness in the stories of the survivors. Here, however, I wish to refer instead to the title of one of Hannah Arendt's essays on the holocaust entitled, "The Perfect Meaninglessness [*Die vollendete Sinnlosigkeit*]."[11] Already in *The Origins of Totalitarianism*, she had made the point that economically speaking, the concentrations camps were useless, pointless, and "existed mostly for their own sake."[12] The Nazis, she writes here, "carried this uselessness to the point of open anti-utility" when on Himmler's direct order neither economic nor military considerations were to detract from the goal of the complete extermination of Jews.[13] Arendt characterizes this obvious contradiction between the holocaust and the necessities of the war activities as a "mad unreality," and she speaks of the "concentration-camp society" as an "insane" world, as "a place where senselessness is daily produced anew."[14] Even though the extermination of the Jews severely affected the German labor force and thus the military requirements for the conduct of war, it had priority over all economic and military necessities. Considering the industrial complex repeated protests, the deportation of Jews fit for work highlights the extent to which the plan for their eradication was nonsensical because, after all, the Nazis also wanted to win the war. But as Dan Diner adds, by annulling the very foundations of rationality conceived in a utilitarian and instrumentalitarian perspective, the Nazis transgressed, at the same time, "the absolute validity of self-preservation—the self-preservation of those responsible" for the crimes.[15] The senselessness of the death camps is thus further increased by its *Zweckwidrigkeit*. In addition, it is well established that the extermination was not to come to a stop once all the Jews, gypsies, homosexuals, and so forth had been liquidated. Hitler anticipated "an auto-genocide far more significant than that of the Jews," once the war was over: up to three quarters of the German newborns were to be assassinated to secure a truly pure race.[16] In all regards, the factual extermination in the camps of a large segment of humanity is incomprehensible, and even more so if it is seen against the plans in their entirety. As the historian Christian Meier notes: "Probably no other event in history offers such radical resistance to every attempt to uncover some meaning in it."[17] It is a totally senseless event, and, therefore, all the more terrible. Even though, in *The Origins of Totalitarianism*, Arendt is led to assume a kind of "supersense [*eine Art Suprasinn*]" of the destruction of all interconnected meaning—namely, totalitarianism's "ideological superstition"—from which even the most absurd activities and institutions receive their meaning, the phantasm of total domination that, according to Arendt, the Nazi pursued, does not make this "supersense" less senseless.[18] On the contrary! It clearly follows from this that the story of the event in question cannot be told, if a story is indeed a form by which events are interlaced so as to become meaningful.

When we speak of the holocaust, we do so in general by way of categories (or images) that thoroughly miss the nature of the event, categories that we use in the average to orient ourselves in the world, and to make sense of it. But in the case of an event as abnormal as the holocaust, these categories are simply inadequate, if not even inappropriate. It should therefore also be clear that I am talking here of an incomprehensibility and senselessness that is not simply beyond everyday experience, or even beyond the grasp of rational thought. To associate it with irrationality is to still approach this senselessness from within the horizon of reason. But as Arendt's observations on the complete disregard of the planned final solution for all economic and military considerations demonstrate, the senselessness is rather one of utter a-rationality: it is a senselessness for its own sake. Hence, the high degree of calculation that characterizes it and that makes of it an intolerable and revolting senselessness.

✦ ✦ ✦

If the specificity of the gruesome horror of what occurred in Auschwitz is linked to its utter senselessness, then this linkage warrants a series of cautionary remarks. Linking the two is, inevitably, a way of making sense of the enormity of the crime. But in order for this sense not to diminish the horrendousness of the event, it is necessary to resist several temptations. Schematically speaking, the first temptation consists of reducing the phenomenal component of the death camps—the wanton brutality with which the inmates were treated, the methodic starvation, the gas chambers, and so forth—to manageable proportions. For example, one may attempt to render it comprehensible by invoking an inclination of the Germans to authoritarian rule, or their ingrained predisposition to bestiality and sadism, which, if it is not held to be part of their natural constitution, is seen as the result of their cultural formation by a tradition—ultimately, Western—which, as some hold, has been intrinsically racist since its origins in Greece. The second temptation concerns the senselessness of the crimes. Specifically, it consists of turning the very senselessness of the crimes into sense itself, whether, by conceiving of their senselessness and pointlessness as a supra-sense, or by labeling the harrowing crimes "the holocaust." Both types of temptation are, in a way, inevitable if the name "Auschwitz" denotes an event so monstrous and senseless as to be unheard of, and which, for this very reason, demands to be understood.

This demand for comprehension is all the more pressing since the terrifying brutality and magnitude of the crime are such that it becomes senseless, and this senselessness, with all its (calculated) arbitrariness, is precisely what makes it so horrifying. But by giving into the temptations in question, the horrendousness and senselessness of Auschwitz are cut into manageable proportions.

To resist such reduction, it is necessary to elaborate on the modality of the link between the very horrific nature of the event—Auschwitz—and its senselessness. If the horror of Auschwitz is not to be tempered by explanations of it on the basis of human cruelty or perversion, or by the discovery of some supra-sense in its senselessness, it follows that no (dialectical) reconciliation between its terrifying brutality and its senselessness can be allowed to mitigate the tension between the two dimensions of the crime. The horror and the senselessness of the event Auschwitz must remain in a relation of paradox, or better, of aporia, in order for both to make sense without making sense, and hence without stripping the event of its outrageousness regarding both its unspeakable brutality and essential senselessness.

How then to conceive of the horrific senselessness of Auschwitz without its sense effacing its senselessness? It must be noted, first, that the harrowing crime is not simply to be measured by the victims' subjective incomprehension of what they experienced, because the extermination was also objectively senseless in economic, military, and all other respects. Even if Auschwitz is, as it is here, the name for what was the ultimate goal of all the other camps—namely, the complete annihilation of all Jews, gypsies, and homosexuals, among many others—this goal does not give what occurred there its definitive and determined sense. On the contrary! Even conceptually speaking, the *Endlösung*, the final solution by way of the extermination of all Jews, gypsies, homosexuals, etc., is a liquidation of sense itself. As the term "ex-termination" suggests, it consists of a driving out of something or someone not simply from established boundaries, but also from its own bounds, hence totally destroying or liquidating it like an enemy or some pest. But "ex-termination" also means to relieve something of its end, to bring the end in which it finds its sense to an end, and thus to liquidate its sense. But, furthermore, "extermination" as a final solution means, in Jean-Luc Nancy's words, "to abolish the very access to the *end*, to liquidate sense [...] as if sense, or existence, were ready to *finish themselves off*, in order to do away with the *end* that was proper to them."[19] Consequently, qua final solution, the event called "Auschwitz" amounts to a liquidation in which its victims undertake their self-liquidation, abolishing themselves the sense proper to them. The specificity of the final solution called "Auschwitz" crystallizes as this attempt to abolish its own meaning by implicating the self-liquidation of its victims' sense as Jews, gypsies, homosexuals, etc. This senselessness of the holocaust, if it is thought without compromise—in other words, in all its incommensurability—is what makes the crimes perpetrated at Auschwitz distinct from all other previous crimes in the history of humanity. And yet, the uniqueness of this event begs to be understood, inevitably in ways that entail comparisons, precedents, generalities, despite the fact that to understand it one must abstain from these, as they diminish its senselessness by making sense of it.

If what distinguishes it from other crimes against humanity is its intrinsic senselessness, Auschwitz can nevertheless not, strictly speaking, be determined in terms of a specificity that would be particular to it (alone). To do so would first of all imply a comparison of what happened there with other, earlier or later, abominations, and would imply that it is a species or genre of atrocity, possibly a genre of atrocity all by itself in which it would be included as this genre's sole case. But if one takes seriously the senselessness that characterizes it, this senselessness defies the possibility of bestowing on Auschwitz the unity of a genre, or species. All comparisons of the holocaust with other previous or later events, however necessary they may be to make sense of it, suggest that there is a common measure against which it can be held and evaluated. But apart from making the holocaust commensurable in this manner, and thus giving it a significance in terms of which it is only distinct by a degree from previous atrocities, the inherent senselessness of the holocaust precludes the assumption of a standard. In view of this senselessness one may wish to speak of it as a horribleness that is unlike all other abominations, comparable to none other before it.

How then is one to think of a horror whose horrendousness is due to its senselessness—a horror that for this very reason cannot be categorized as having a tragic nature? Can one speak of such a horrendousness that defies comparison in terms of what Kierkegaard calls the "truly horrifying," "most terrible," or the "truly appalling"?[20] If such an understanding of the terrible in a superlative sense is framed by ethico-religious considerations, as is the case with Kierkegaard, a superlative horror makes the incommensurability of the terrible eminently meaningful. For the same reasons that the holocaust must be, but also cannot be compared to any other crimes without reducing its singularity, it also cannot be construed as a superlative of heinousness. Any such attempt presupposes a framework with respect to which the horror is made commensurable.

However, in the case of Auschwitz we face a horror whose incomprehensibility is based on the fact that it fits no standard, and of whose measurelessness (being out of proportion to any other crime) no measure can make sense. Rather than making sense of the holocaust by calling it an utterly senseless event, the conclusion that the very senselessness of Auschwitz is of such a nature as to defy all possible intelligibility avoids both the surrender of understanding and the delegation of its intelligibility to a power higher than that of the finite human being. On the contrary, it is a way of doing justice to the contradictory character of the event whose extreme nature demands to be understood but that at the same time defies understanding, not because only a God can make sense of it within the framework of a hidden plan of salvation, but because the nature of the event called "Auschwitz" is such that it destroys any sense that could be imparted to it.

✦ ✦ ✦

But is such senselessness, then, of the order of the "unimaginable"? In response to this question, it should suffice to recall what Robert Antelme says about this word to describe the horrors of the camps: "*Unimaginable*: a word that doesn't divide, doesn't restrict. The most convenient word. When you walk around with this word as your shield, this word for emptiness, your step becomes better assured, more resolute, your conscience pulls itself together."[21]

✦ ✦ ✦

Undoubtedly, to contend that the abomination of the horrors of Auschwitz is a function of its ultimate senselessness may seem to be counterintuitive. It may even appear shocking, if not insensitive, to assert that the meaning or signification of Auschwitz is not arrested or saturated by the fact that its aim was purely and simply to eliminate an entire race. But let us remind ourselves here of the imperative and unavoidable Fregian distinction between sense and meaning (i.e., reference, or signification). If what happened at Auschwitz remains incomprehensible even to those who survived its atrocities, it is because the event in question is not exhausted by its possible subjugation to a definite meaning. Or rather, however evident its meaning or signification, it does not make sense. But if it is impossible to make sense of even an evident meaning of Auschwitz, such as the complete extermination of the Jews, Auschwitz is nevertheless not unintelligible. There is a logic, a structure to its horrors, a sense, a *Sinn*, in short, (in distinction from its *Bedeutung*), which makes its senselessness intelligible. If in spite of the utter senselessness of its horrors, what happened in the death camps must nonetheless be understood, such understanding cannot consist in converting this senselessness into some determined meaning, but rather in rendering it intelligible without reducing its horrors to an evident, although aberrant meaning.[22] Or could it be that, in this case, we are dealing with a senselessness in which the distinction between sense and meaning has been weakened, blurred, or perverted? Would one not even be forced to consider the possibility that the intention of Auschwitz was to irremediably destroy the possibility of distinguishing between its sense and its meaning, and thus the possibility of making sense of its lack of meaning? But even in the case of such an extreme possibility, the demand to understand still remains intact. It would still be necessary to inquire into how this blurring is effectuated and what kind of logic informs it, or in other words, what sense it has.

✦ ✦ ✦

A senselessness such as that of the grueling reality of the death camps instills muteness in its victims. Certainly this muteness can be the effect of a traumatic impairment of memory, for example, but, in essence, this inability to tell stories has deeper, if not structural, reasons. Only something as senseless as the horror of Auschwitz causes, with a certain necessity that is not simply empirical, an inevitable muteness. To understand it, rather than searching for physiological, psychological, or traumatic reasons, requires dwelling on the horrors that lead to it, to which muteness is, no doubt, if not the sole, a possible response.

Seeking to understand rather than justify the specific reasons for the collectivization in the Soviet Union which caused the inhumane repression—through executions and deportation of the *koulaks*—Georges Bataille argues that "in view of this end [that is, the collectivization] it seems superficial to dwell lengthily on the horrors."[23] However, in *The Origins of Totalitarianism*, Hannah Arendt argues that, on the contrary, if the concentration camps, whether those of Nazi Germany or the Soviet Union, are "the most consequential institution of totalitarian rule," "'dwelling on horrors' would seem to be indispensable for the understanding of totalitarianism."[24] But she also points out that such dwelling cannot take place adequately by way of memoirs or testimonies. The latter, she holds, remain within the order of "statements of common sense, whether of a psychological nature, [and only] serve to encourage those who think it 'superficial' to 'dwell on horrors.'"[25] She adds that, indeed,

> recollection can no more do this [that is, "dwell on horrors"] than can the uncommunicative eyewitness report. In both these genres there is an inherent tendency to run away from the experience; instinctively or rationally, both types of writer are so much aware of the terrible abyss that separates the world of the living from that of the living dead, that they cannot supply anything more than a series of remembered occurrences that must seem just as incredible to those who relate them as to their audience. Only the *fearful imagination* of those who have been aroused by such reports but have not actually been smitten in their own flesh, of those who are consequently free from the bestial, desperate terror which, when confronted by real, present horror, inexorably paralyzes everything that is not mere reaction, can afford to keep thinking about horrors.[26]

The living dead in the camps experienced these horrors in their own flesh to a degree that, even when they survived the camps, they were paralyzed to such an extent that their testimony and memories could not express them. By contrast, those who have not actually experienced the horrors in question, but who, because of the memoirs and accounts of those who have been its victims are forced to represent them to themselves, are capable of dwelling on them precisely because they themselves have not been affected by them. But only the "fearful imagination" of those aroused by the reports is capable of lingering on the horrors in question. Undoubtedly, Arendt's conception of the imagination as a power that by keeping a certain distance to what otherwise would overwhelm and paralyze our faculties of judgment, explains her reference to the faculty in question as the only one permitted to linger on the horrors. But only a "fearful imagination" is capable of such a task. How are we to understand this expression?

Since in her own translation of *The Origins of Totalitarianism* into German—a translation that, as Arendt admits, is not always literally faithful to the original—the author abandons the reference to a fearful imagination and replaces it with the expression "anticipating fear [*antizipierende Angst*]"—it is most likely that Arendt did not have a technical philosophical conception of the imagination in mind when she used the English expression. Indeed, the expression "a fearful imagination" is most likely a translation of the German "eine erschreckte Einbildungskraft," which, notwithstanding its rarity, is not an altogether uncommon expression.[27] And yet, given the context in the original in which she appeals to a "fearful imagination," could one not venture to suggest that this notion has a certain potential to address what has happened to a faculty such as the imagination of victims smitten with the horrors on which they cannot dwell? Is a "fearful [*erschreckte*] imagination" not also one that has been paralyzed and stifled by what it beholds, and that, because it can no longer keep intact the distance required for it to represent its object, reduces the subject to muteness?[28] Indeed, in the face of the complete senselessness of the horror that Auschwitz stands for, the imagination is paralyzed because, in Kantian terms, it can no longer accomplish the sensible synthesis of what it is confronted with, and, hence, of making sense of it. The imagination is not only frightened by the unimaginable and senseless horrors that face it, and therefore unable to synthesize them tangibly into stories. From an Aristotelian point of view, the horrendousness of the event—the holocaust—also frightens the imagination because it is terrified by the possibility of rendering again as fully present what is no longer present—that is, of bringing to life again, and hence in a way reenacting the enormity of the crime. An imagination terrified by the enormity of the senseless horror is an imagination that condemns all the other powers of the mind to silence, or rather to muteness.

✦ ✦ ✦

It is certainly possible to provide information regarding this senselessness and to be a witness of it. But can it therefore be shaped into the form of a story without making sense of what happened in the death camps, and thus taking the unimaginable terror out of it? The survivors' notorious muteness regarding their experiences is not only testimony to the need not to confuse this inability to tell their stories in living voice with the two other activities—namely, those of providing information or testifying to what happened, but also, of the necessity of telling the story of what they underwent—a necessity exemplified by the urge, despite the impossibility of conveying such experiences in a verbal form, to do so in a written form. Chil Rajchman's memoir on the Treblinka death camp is dedicated to "all those to whom it was not possible to tell this tale" in living voice, including his own brother, the only other survivor of his family, to whom he did not speak about his life as a prisoner in the camp, but to whom, significantly enough, a while after their reunion, he gave written notes about his time there.[29] The recourse to writing about the plight in which the prisoners in the camps found themselves is not a way of overcoming of their muteness, but rather presupposes and confirms it. Although certainly untellable because too painful to remember, but especially due to the lack of all meaning regarding what happened in the death camps, the impossible story of the camps nevertheless has to be formed and, wherever possible, told again and again, and always in a new way, even at the price of mitigating the event's radical evil by giving it form, the form of a story, as long as it remains clear that no story is capable of making sense of it. But the sheer nonsensical reality of the monstrous horror of the exterminations needs to be recognized without compromise before it can be shaped into a story. In her conversation with Günter Gaus, Arendt observes that what happened in Auschwitz is something "to which we cannot reconcile ourselves," and that although she could accept everything else, she never would be able to accept what happened there. This, perhaps, is not so much because "the fabrication of corpses" in Auschwitz is "something completely different," but rather because it was entirely incomprehensible given its inherent absurdity.[30] To reconcile oneself with Auschwitz would mean having found a meaning in it—in short, a story. One further difficulty that arises with the systematic and, at the same time, senseless extermination of the Jews, is that even though it is "a universal simile" as Imre Kertesz has argued, the holocaust is an event utterly without a lesson.[31] Stories, as will be seen in due time, are not only forms of intelligence, but forms that have a practical purpose: they make a coup by giving counsel. However, in the holocaust there is no lesson to be found and consequently, no lesson to be told. Suffice it to quote Ruth Klüger who writes that

> Auschwitz was no instructional institution [...] You learned nothing there, at least of all humanity and tolerance. Absolutely nothing good came out of the concentration camps [...] They were the most useless, pointless establishments imaginable. That is the one thing to remember about them if you know nothing else.[32]

If by contrast Auschwitz has become a "universal simile," and "a universal experience," in that it is "the most traumatic event in Western civilization," is it precisely not because the horrendous senselessness of what happened there has no possible moral lesson or meaning but, on the contrary, amounts to the bankruptcy of ethics in general.[33] Indeed, the fact that such a thing was possible has forever affected the foundations—metaphysical, humanist, and theological—on which Western ethics, at least, has been based. But as the reference to a "universal simile" suggests, its consequences reverberate well beyond the West.

The survivors' notorious muteness, their inability to shape into the form of a story what happened in the camps and what they underwent there, is in the last instance to be retraced to the senselessness in question, which has impaired their ability to understand what happened to them. In addition to the senseless horror they suffered, they underwent an experience that made the process of making sense of what happened to them by rendering it in the form of a story senseless as well.

✦ ✦ ✦

In the camps, as Klüger confides,

> the thought already occurred to her, a thought that unfortunately sits deeper in her than the outrage about the enormous crime, namely the consciousness of the absurdity of the whole thing, its nonsensical

> nature, the complete senselessness of these murders and deportations that we call the final solution, the Jewish catastrophe, the Holocaust, and nowadays the Shoah, always new names, because words for the crimes in question rapidly rot in our mouth.[34]

Indeed, all of these notions, the one of the holocaust in particular, give the event a definite meaning that makes it intelligible, alleviating the event of the horrifying nature of its senselessness. First used by Elie Wiesel, the name "holocaust" as a name for the final solution has been questioned by several of the survivors themselves. Among them is Levi, who termed it unacceptable since the notion interprets the extermination of the Jews in the camps as a punishment for their sins.[35] As a euphemism, the biblical term "Shoah," meaning "calamity" or "catastrophe," which in the Scriptures is also often linked to the idea of a divine punishment, might perhaps be less divisive, as Agamben suggests, especially if the term is understood as saying more, and something other than "genocide," speaking of all the inmates of the camps.[36] Thus understood, the term "Shoah," as Jean-Luc Nancy submits, is possibly not a word for the unnamable but only a "breath," "an enormous murmur" in relation to "the vile [*infâme*]: the unspeakable, proclaimed, or renamed," an expression of lament which, as Benjamin notes, "contains scarcely more than the sensuous breath [*sinnlichen Hauch*]."[37]

Until now I too have referred to what happened in the extermination camps as the "holocaust," and will continue to do so for reasons of convenience. But at no moment should we lose sight of the fact that what was done to the inmates in the death camps made no sense, and that a term such as "holocaust" serves to reduce the senselessness of the extermination, and, by the same token, what made this event so monstrous. Calling the event "holocaust" is a way of appropriating it for purposes extrinsic to the suffering of the victims. If many of the survivors of the final solution returned mute, unable to tell their stories, it is also because what they underwent can no longer be called an "experience." What they lived through, which can perhaps be circumscribed by way of the German word "Erlebnis" (lived experience, as it is usually translated), is an experience which, in distinction from the one termed "Erfahrung," is not defined by sense and cannot therefore be communicated in the form of sense that is a story because it is no longer an experience. To label the victims "holocaust survivors" is to turn their lack of an experience into one at the cost of attenuating their deprivation of an experience to begin with. A term such as "holocaust" gives to what had no sense whatsoever a definite religious meaning. It converts the senseless into a figure of sense.

❖ ❖ ❖

In order for their stories not to be forgotten once they have passed away, some of the survivors of the nuclear attacks at Hiroshima and Nagasaki, whose numbers are rapidly dwindling, have designated a "denshosha"—that is, a transmitter of their memories—to preserve their stories and keep them alive once they themselves are no longer able to pass them on. Yet such an attempt to preserve the memories of the victims of the bomb is possible only because having already told their stories has made it possible for others to become the heirs of their recollections. But as a result of World War I, a new and highly disturbing phenomenon had already emerged in Europe—namely, that of soldiers returning from the front unable to speak about what they had witnessed. Their case in particular is a familiar one because Sigmund Freud's work on war and traumatic neuroses led him to develop his metapsychological theory of the death drive. But since I am concerned here with storytelling, I rather wish to evoke Walter Benjamin's reference in "The Storyteller" to the men who returned from the battlefield not simply having grown silent, as the English translation has it, but having grown mute (*verstummt*). As a symptom of the process of the loss of experience that began to become apparent with World War I, the returning soldier's muteness was not the result of their deliberate choice, but rather of something that happened to them. One of its causes, Benjamin submits, was that they returned from war "not richer but poorer in communicable experience"—in short, "as if a capability that seemed inalienable [*unveräusserlich*] [...], the securest among our possessions, ha[d] been taken from [them]; the ability to share experiences."[38] If the events they experienced muted their ability to communicate them, it is precisely because these events inhibited the formation of experiences. Benjamin writes:

> For never has experience been more thoroughly belied than strategic experience was belied by tactical warfare, economic experience by inflation, bodily experience by mechanical warfare, moral experience by those in power. A generation that had gone to school on horse-drawn streetcars now stood under the open sky in a landscape where nothing remained unchanged but the clouds and, beneath those clouds, in a force field of destructive torrents and explosions, the tiny, fragile human body.[39]

What thus had muted the soldiers who returned from war was the complete destruction of the fabric of relations that existed between men (as well as between men and animals), which until then had made it possible to exchange experiences. As a result of this destruction of the interrelational web between human beings, the soldiers became not only isolated from one another as individuals, but also demoted to miniscule and frail human bodies. The destructive material forces to which they were thus exposed and under which they passively lived

(*Erlebnisse*), deprived them of the possibility of making any communicable experiences (*Erfahrungen*).

If in the following I am interested primarily in the holocaust survivors' notorious silence, or rather their muteness in regard to the horrendous things they lived through in camps, it is not in order to minimize other events that resulted in human beings having been condemned to muteness. The priority that, admittedly, I attribute to the holocaust in this study derives, first and foremost, from the fact that its victims were the objects of a systematic and concerted effort on the part of its perpetrators to induce the victims' muteness. The atrocities that the warring parties in World War I and those responsible for other terrible events that have happened in the past—such as the Armenian genocide, the "forgotten" genocide of the Herero and Namaqua by the Germans in Namibia, for example, and since the holocaust, the mass killings of the Kmer Rouge, the Rwandan Genocide, the ethnic cleansing in Croatia, to name only a few, and, at this very moment, the persecution of the Rohingya in Myanmar—inflicted on their victims, do not compare to what occurred in the extermination camps, because these other atrocities were not predominately and purposively machinated with this goal in mind.

Given that to generalize implies passing from like to like—that is, by holding the phenomena under consideration as alike in most respects—the current trend, in the name of what has become known as "the syndrome of the survivor," at an ahistorical leveling out of the holocaust, warrants a couple of further remarks about the priority that I accord to the latter in this study about its survivors' muteness. Needless to say, the topic of this study requires a concentration on this specific event and also, given the reading of Benjamin's "The Storyteller" that I provide, a comparison with the returning soldiers' muteness after World War I. But the point I wish to make is that the syndrome of the survivor abstracts from the singularity of what happened in the case of the holocaust, an abstraction that does injustice not only to the specificity of what the holocaust victims suffered, but also to all the victims of all past and present genocides or mass exterminations. Undoubtedly, the notion of syndrome and the psychic trace of the drama to which it refers, traumatism, in short, makes it possible for the victims to earn social recognition. However, such recognition comes with a price, which is paid by no other than the victims themselves, for indeed each of these horrific events that they have undergone is unique. To deny anyone of the originality of what they underwent amounts to an aseptic packaging of the horrors in all their concrete historical reality. However, to insist on the irreducible originality of each of the horrendous events in question does not mean that no comparison is possible between them, and that nothing universal can be made out about them, but only that this cannot be a generality that levels the differences between all these events. Judging that an event of this sort is unique implies that it is repeatable, that it has predecessors, and that in the future similar events are possible, otherwise the very uniqueness of the unique horrendous event itself would altogether be unintelligible.

As I have said, the context of this study requires a prime focus on the holocaust, a prioritization of it in order to explain the mutism of so many of its survivors. But in order to account for this mutism I also prioritize the holocaust, in that I hold that something unique was engineered here that had not taken place before in the same way and that perhaps has not yet been repeated on other similar occasions.[40] As Didier Fassin and Richard Rechtman have convincingly shown in their archaeological inquiry into the nosological category of traumatism and the politics associated with this category, a certain interpretation of the Shoah has played a crucial role in the generalization of the condition of the victim and the formation of a universal language to secure the recognizability of victimhood.[41] If the holocaust has thus enjoyed a priority, as Fassin and Rechtman demonstrate, it is first of all because it is this event which has given rise in the United States during the eighties of the past century—that is, with a significant, if not telling belatedness—to a problematics and its sustaining concepts, which today are at the heart of the discussion of violence in a broader historical and worldwide context. However necessary and laudable such awareness is, it is not therefore innocent. Generalizing the victim's condition as simply one of traumatism amounts to denying the specificity of the holocaust and making what happened in this case, and in the same breadth, in other cases, trite.[42] But if the holocaust enjoyed this questionable priority in a theory intended on equalizing victimhood, is it not precisely in order to avoid recognizing the very disturbing uniqueness of what took place there to begin with.[43]

After the cosmological, biological, and psychological injuries to the human being's self-love, of which Freud speaks, the phenomenon of Auschwitz in a culture such as Europe that perceived itself as a high culture, not only added a final injury to all the previous ones, but this one particular injury, no doubt, represented for European humanity the very mark of its complete demise. For indeed the violence associated in the heart of Europe with the extermination of the Jews especially, but other ethnicities as well, not only put into question all of Europe's cultural and spiritual accomplishment, especially the values regarding the essence of what is human, but also consisted in a violence in which reason—the very mark of Europe—is put into the service of eliminating reason itself in a systematic—that is, rational fashion. No wonder, therefore, that the holocaust is understood not only as a horrific extermination of entire peoples, and in the same breath of all of European values, but as the profound destruction of reason by way of its instrumentalization for the benefit of non-reason. This is what gives the holocaust a status that is unique in that apart from the kind of violence involved in it, it consisted in an attempt to destroy not simply the rational foundations of European humanity as a whole, but of reason itself, something that is not something exclusively European, but also concerns whatever functions as a principle of intelligibility in all other, non-Western cultures.

For the problematic that I pursue in this essay the priority that I give to the holocaust and its victims is based on still another feature of this horrific and senseless event. It concerns the muteness with which it struck its victims. Undoubtedly, elements of what happened in the extermination camps during World War II including organized violence directed toward the erasure of any possibility of remembrance are present in earlier and later events of organized violence. It remains, however, that this feature of a concerted pursuit of erasure of memory, and in the same breath, the effort of muting possible survivors, is a pervasive feature of the holocaust without which it cannot adequately be historically determined. The holocaust took place by the "Nacht und Nebel (by night and fog)" decree. For this reason, one could argue that the only mass exterminations, with which it might be compared are the forgotten genocides.

Since it is my intention to inquire into the impossibility of why so many survivors of the holocaust were unable to tell their stories, I must, needless to say, privilege this particular occurrence of senseless violence. What then constitutes in this context the specificity of the holocaust? First, let me point out that besides the much discussed industrialized form of extermination involved, the state-organized violence against the Jews (and other minorities) was not a merely local event. The originality of the holocaust is its global nature: the diasporic people were hunted down throughout Europe and beyond. This is not only a consequence of the however perverted instrumentalization of reason for the extermination, but of a purification of race beyond all borders, and which, as we know, was not even to come to a stop before the German people themselves. One touches here at a dimension of what happened in the extermination camps that is not of the order of an accident, but that characterizes the event in its entirety giving it a metaphysical status, as it were. It is not just a senseless undertaking in all respects, it is an attempt at a systematic perversion of reason in the European sense, but beyond it of any principle that gives sense to the world and its history. What distinguishes the holocaust from perhaps all other historical occurrences of mass exterminations is this underlying metaphysical agenda to which, furthermore, large segments of the intellectual class in Germany lent their hand. This needs to remain present to our mind in assessing the issue of its survivors' muteness, which is the inevitable result of the concerted effort to globally destroy any principle of intelligibility, whether called by its European name or by the name it has in other cultures.

At this juncture I wish to return to those numerous holocaust survivors who have been unable to speak about their experiences in the camps even to their own, closest, family members. Would one not be inclined to think that the horrific conditions they underwent and witnessed would be reason enough for them to speak profusely about them? And if, indeed, what the inmates of the death camps experienced was beyond imagination and unsayable, would one not therefore expect them to feel the necessity and urgency to speak and to testify about it? But of his stay in Auschwitz, Tadeusz Borowski remarks that "[y]our memory retains only images" of it to which one certainly can think back and perhaps describe, but such images are not communicable experiences.[44] So what about the unwillingness, refusal, or rather inability of many survivors to speak about the "hell" they survived? What does their silence or rather muteness mean?

Some may object to this concern with the victims' muteness, arguing that many of them have spoken by testifying to what happened in the camps, and that, hence, they were not mute. Furthermore, they may evoke the stories that a number of the victims have provided in writing. Considering these facts, the importance given here to muteness is out of proportion with the survivors' testimony—an exaggeration of sorts. But do testifying and telling stories not remain distinct activities? Telling stories in a living voice and in writing: aren't these different things as well? But if one acknowledges that, indeed, many of the survivors not only wrote memoirs because they could not tell their stories, but did not even speak to their family members about what life in the camps was like, is muteness then not a phenomenon with respect to which exaggeration is inevitable, but that also demands a certain methodic overemphasis in order to be brought to light or to the stage in the first place? If not overstated, the victims' muteness might remain inaudible, incapable of being identified and understood.[45] Such overemphasis is needed in order to save the phenomenon not, however, by explaining it as the classical formula "saving the phenomena" demands, but more paradoxically, by honoring the *skandalon* involved by its refusal to be rendered meaningful.

Several of the survivors who have written on the life in the camps have emphasized the extent to which storytelling was part of whatever social activity was still permitted. Borowski reports that "[e]verybody here tells stories—on the way to work, returning to the camp, working in the fields and in the trucks, in the bunks at night, standing at roll-call. Stories from books and stories from life. And almost always about the world outside the barbed-wire fence."[46] No doubt, in the context of the death camps, such frenzied storytelling is a way of warding off or forestalling death, not unlike Scheherazade's effort in the *Arabian Nights* of postponing her own death from one morning to another. Primo Levi, for his part, evokes the painful, cruel, and moving stories, numbering "hundreds of thousands of stories, all different," which the inmates "told to one another in the evening," and which were "simple and incomprehensible, like the stories in the Bible."[47]

This frenzy of storytelling, however, could be seen as one response or reaction to what constituted the center of the death camps, from which the remaining population of the camps—constantly terrorized by the specter of "the Muselmann who at every moment was emerging within [them]"— sought to distinguish themselves at all costs.[48] Against the presence of non-humans, not only without a face, but also without a voice, the profuse telling of stories whenever possible not only served as a way to ward off the always immanent threat of being selected for the gas chambers, but also as a way to retain at least a minimum amount of dignity and respect. Telling their stories to one another, the detainees sought to resist the complete divestment of their humanity. Compared to the stories continuously told in the camps—stories, as Levi says, that were "incomprehensible, like the stories in the Bible," and whose inherent sense was therefore already fading—the returning survivors' silence is, therefore, all the more striking, and it suggests that this is not just any silence and that the refusal to speak, or the inability to do so, requires an approach other than finding plausible reasons for it. It is a silence that cannot simply be explained and therein reduced by weighty reasons to comfortable proportions. For the same reason this silence, more precisely, this muteness, cannot be judged to be something that is in the power of the survivors and could, therefore, be held as a (violent) omission of sorts in relation to those who lived in safety. A remark in the opening lines of Robert Antelme's *The Human Race* is highly significant in this context. He reports that in the first days following their liberation, all the returnees

> were prey to a genuine delirium. We wanted at last to speak, to be heard [...] we felt a frantic desire to describe it such as it had been. As

> of those first days, however, we saw that it was impossible to bridge the gap we discovered opening up between the words at our disposal and that experience which, in the case of most of us, was still going forward within our bodies [...] No sooner would we begin to tell our story than we would be choking over it [*que nous suffoquions*]. And then, even to us, what we had to tell would start to seem unimaginable.[49]

The very nature of what the inmates of the camps experienced, for which the word "unimaginable" serves as a protective shield, inhibits its communication. Face to face with the American soldiers who liberated them, the survivor, Antelme reports, sensed "welling up within him a feeling that he is from now on going to be prey to a kind of infinite, untransmittable knowledge."[50] In short, the frantic desire of the survivors to tell what happened to them ushers in muteness, and when they do, in fact, succeed in telling their stories, their inherent reservations prevent them from being the stories as they continue to pursue them in their bodies. This muteness that underlies what is finally told is also something that the survivors do not have the power to change. The elucidation from various angles of the implications of this muteness that I am concerned with hereafter proceeds on the recognition of the survivors' taciturnity as an irreducible phenomenon. This phenomenon must be respected as such.

In the considerable literature that has been devoted to the survivors' "refusal" to testify to their ordeals, many factors have been shown to be involved: on a discursive level, the witnesses' silence has been attributed to their incapacity to say the unsayable; to the limits of representing the unrepresentable; or to the failure of the imagination to capture the horrific reality of life in the camps. To all of this, let us also add their failure to meet the standards of cognitive proof.[51] On a sociocultural level, this impossibility to tell can be retraced to feelings of guilt, or shame of having survived, and, even in the case of Jews, who were the majority of the inmates, the fear of unleashing further anti-Semitism. On a psychiatrical and especially psychoanalytical level, what needs mentioning is trauma theory, which casts the wounds inflicted on the minds of the holocaust survivors and their symptoms in terms a pathological condition or psychic disorder.[52] Undoubtedly, the survivors' inability to tell their stories is a multifaceted, highly complex phenomenon, and cannot be retraced to a simple cause. But whatever the individual and concrete reasons for the victim's silence, the phenomenon of their muteness—and perhaps also of the muteness that pervades the accounts given by those who seemingly were able to speak[53]—begs to be understood in itself, in its significance and implications, independently of its multiple possible reasons. Indeed, whatever its specific causes and its degrees are, the victims' muteness suggests that something has irrevocably happened to what Benjamin called the seemingly inalienable capacity of sharing one's story by telling it, something that cannot exhaustively (or at all) be explained by these causes alone. Yet, if this is the case, what are the ultimate consequences of not being able to speak about what happened to oneself, more precisely, of not being able to tell one's story to others? If furthermore, even those who spoke about their experiences might not really have said anything, what is one to draw from this impossibility? For indeed, if those who spoke did so, it is, as Primo Levi suggests, because they had been invited to do so. But more often than not the questions to which they were supposed to respond were framed already in such a way that they contained the wished response, demonstrating a complete lack of understanding on the part of the questioner of what human beings, rather than an abstract concept such as "totalitarianism," did in the camps to other human beings, Jews and non-Jews alike.[54] As Imre Kertesz forcefully notes in *Fatelessness*, by his interlocutor's preference to speak about the camps as hell, or as a place where atrocities however unspeakable were committed, the survivor is invited to respond to clichés by way of other clichés.[55] In light of what the detainees of the death camps underwent, all representations or characterizations appear unfit. Furthermore, what Giorgio Agamben has called "the aporia of Auschwitz," consists precisely in the irreducibility of the reality of Auschwitz—that is, of what the victims and survivors underwent, to even the factual elements of Auschwitz.[56] Even the facts are insufficient to describe the reality in question: facts and truth, verification and comprehension, do not coincide in this case. If stories, then, are not sufficient ways of telling what happened in the camps because the situation there was of the order of the unspeakable, beyond imagination and representation—what I have called "senseless" as such—with the result that, in Levi's words, "a memory that is recollected too often, and expressed in the form of a story, tends to harden into a stereotype, a tried-and-true formula, crystallized, perfected, adorned, that installs itself in the place of raw memory and grows at its expense," it follows that the reality of the camps has affected and might, at the limit, have destroyed the seemingly fundamental human ability of telling stories, especially one's own, and, by the same token, the faculty of relating to others.[57] If this assumption is correct, what are the ramifications? The survivors' inability to tell their stories—in Kertesz's words, their inability to "give orders to memory"[58]— seems to thoroughly have put into question Isak Dinesen's claim that "[a]ll sorrows can be borne if you put them into a story or tell a story about them."[59] But unless one assumes that by remaining silent about what they underwent in the death camps the detainees in question made the only existential statement possible under the circumstances, by telling others through that very silence that their ability to tell has itself been impaired in a lasting manner, this inability to tell not only amounts to the impossibility of bearing the sorrows in question, but it is ultimately testimony to the destruction of what has been believed to be a basic human condition of identifying oneself through one's stories. If all the reasons mentioned for the detainees' silence, including trauma-induced amnesia, still presuppose some minimal identity of the survivor, a surviving core of selfhood, does an inability of telling one's story not in a way suggest that the sorrows to which Dinesen refers cannot be borne because its subject has been in its very identity structurally damaged? For this very reason, the stories that they prove unable to tell might also no longer be able to be considered *their* stories. The un-tellable stories might no longer be *stories* at all in that their belonging to a subject has been affected.

As Odo Marquard has pointed out,

> only when an unpredictable thing happens to a process governed by natural laws or a planned action do these events have to be told, and can only be conveyed in the form of stories: stories are processes-contrary-events that befall them-mixtures [*Ablauf-Widerfahrnis-Gemische*], that is, action-contrary events that befall it-mixtures [*Handlungs-Widerfahrnis-Gemische*].[60]

At first glance the experiences in the camps would seem to press, therefore, for narration, but if the survivors' experiences were of such a nature that they could not be told—that is, communicated in the form of stories—it follows that what happened to the victims did not conform to the definition of what makes the form of stories possible and their telling inevitable. What cannot be told because it cannot espouse the form of stories might thus also no longer qualify as being of the order of an *experience*.

As is well documented, the Nazis' plan of extermination of the Jews especially, included the subsequent destruction of all traces of the holocaust so as to make it into an event that never happened. The terrible fear of forgetting what occurred at that time is, however, not simply a threat that affects the holocaust as a past event: as Kertesz remarks, this fear accompanied [behaften] the holocaust from the very first moment it was underway and while it was still the exclusive secret of those involved—that is, its victims and executioners.[61] The sheer monstrosity of what occurred in the death camps is at the core of this fear. The fear that such unspeakable horror could be forgotten preceded not only the survivors' concerns with the holocaust, but also the devised forgetting by the Nazi regime which, apart from the planned erasure of all factual traces, also sought to use the incredibility of the perpetrated crimes in question for this very purpose.[62] The way this forgetting was planned began with the way the detainees were treated.[63]

Indeed, a systematic dehumanization and depersonalization of the inmates of the extermination camps by the SS were instrumental to accomplishing what Levi calls "a war against memory."[64] The "offense" by means of which this dehumanization and depersonalization were accomplished consisted, in his words, in "break[ing] the body and soul of those who are drowned, extinguish[ing] them and mak[ing] them abject" not only in the eyes of the perpetrators, but of the victim as well.[65] As a result, it became impossible for the detainees, even when they survived, to wipe out the traces of the offense, which instilled in them feelings of shame for still being alive. Hannah Arendt, in a more systematic vain, notes that "the disintegration of personality" was accomplished in three steps: first through the destruction of the juridical person—in the Nazis' own terms, the individuals' *Entwürdigung*, amounting to a stripping of all dignity—by being arrested without any relation to one's previous actions or opinions; second, through the destruction of the moral person by way of the incarceration in death camps that were entirely cut off from the world; and finally, through the destruction of the individuality and autonomy of the person, a destruction that was accomplished through "permanent and systematically organized torture."[66] The aim of such methodic depersonalization was to dehumanize the victims by reducing them "to the smallest possible denominator of 'identical reactions,'" and "organic life," with the aim of making them into objects of "total subjugation."[67] Stripped of their names, with only a number tattooed into their flesh as a result of which they became countable entities of barely organic life, in no way different from cattle and with nothing remaining of who they had been, the inmates of the camps were no longer to be considered or to consider themselves as persons, or, ultimately, as humans.[68] Arendt speaks of "the monstrous equality" that the reduction of the occupants of the camps to the smallest possible denominator brought about—an equality that for Arendt, as we later see, means of course, the bereavement of their singularity or uniqueness—that is, precisely, of the one feature that makes a human being human.[69] This extreme destitution of human dignity was exemplified by the so-called *Muselmänner* already mentioned, who not only had been made to surrender themselves to their fate: the bare life and muteness to which they were reduced also amounted to a destruction of all basic human abilities, such as being able to see what was being done to them—and thus tell their story—and, consequently, of having a story and an identity to begin with. Of them Levi remarks that they, "the drowned," "accepting the eclipse of the word," are the true witnesses, though they "could not have borne witness, because their death had already begun before the body perished."[70] In other words, they had also already lost their ability to remember, as Levi notes, well before their physical annihilation.[71] But the systematic debilitation and degradation of the detainees were also intended to prevent them, were they accidentally to have survived, from being able to tell their stories. All memory of what happened in the camps was to be destroyed so that for what happened there never was a witness, and hence that what took place there, never did take place. This process culminated in the erasure of the detainees' faculty of remembering.

In light of this attempt to purposefully destroy the inmates' ability to memorize and speak, the silence or muteness of many of those who returned from the camps raises a set of new questions. For example, is this muteness not a kind of self-destruction as Kertesz seems to suggest in *Liquidation*?[72] Or is this silence or muteness due to an impairment more profound than the multiple reasons that are often invoked to explain it, including traumatic amnesia, an impairment, or perhaps a structural refusal to working through (*durcharbeiten*) the resistances that traumatic experience brings with it, and in which process an interpretation of what the survivors underwent could help them overcome their resistances by providing their experiences with a meaning that each could recognize as his or her own? Is it not an irreparable muteness because these survivors have been rendered unable to "give orders to [their] memory," to cite Kertesz one more time, orders not simply to remember, but also to work through what they have undergone? In any event, it is not a muteness that the survivors have deliberately chosen; it is not a muteness that could be reversed, given the right circumstances and the appropriate questions. And, I add, it is as such, and with respect for this irreducible irreparability that the silence or muteness in question must be approached. Only under this condition can it allow one to think not simply of the horror of which it is unable to speak, but also of the disturbing phenomenon that this muteness itself represents. However, in the following I do not pursue this line of inquiry in a direct manner, but choose, on the contrary, a more indirect way by turning to several theories of narration, which perhaps will allow us a glimpse into what silence or muteness regarding one's experiences can mean in this context. I repeat that it is certainly necessary to distinguish between the holocaust victims' inability *to speak* about their experience, *to bear witness* to what happened in the camps, and *to tell their stories*. Each of these three abilities or inabilities takes place in a different register, with respect to dissimilar tasks, and each calls on distinct faculties for their exercise. They differ from each other regarding their capacity of comprehension of the scale or size of what they address, and what ultimately they are to accomplish. Hereafter, I am only concerned with the incapacity of storytelling and seek to formulate the implications that the destruction of this faculty harbors in terms of three different theories, if one takes seriously what they establish about stories and storytelling. In other words, I wish to gauge the inevitable consequences of being robbed of the power to tell stories, particularly one's own story, in terms of these three theories by drawing on their distinct understandings of the precise conditions under which storytelling is possible, becomes a necessity, as well as what happens when these conditions no longer obtain.

According to Hegel, "in German the term for 'history' (*Geschichte*) … combines the objective and the subjective sides: it denotes the actual events (in Latin, *res gestae*) as well as the narration of the events (in Latin, *historiam rerum gestarum*)."[73] If this "union of the two meanings must be regarded as something of a higher order than mere chance"—in other words, if this union bears witness to the speculative nature of the German language (but does the same not also hold true in many other languages?)—it is because the narration of history is co-originary with the happening of world history—that is, the happening of freedom.[74] The speculative nature of the word "history" is indicative of an intrinsic internal relation between both history and its narrative account (regardless of the difference between history and storytelling in what Hegel calls "originary history" and philosophical history). Indeed, as he argues, peoples, nations, and states as world-historical individualities accomplish such identity only in conjunction with the telling of their history, which is thus part and parcel of their constitution. A similar speculative relation exists between becoming a self and the telling of one's story. Indeed, according to the three influential theories on storytelling that are discussed in this text, only a life capable of being told (by oneself or others) accomplishes a recognizable identity. More generally, only a life capable of being narrated is truly a human life. Only its quality of being narrated provides human life with a singular form of ideality, as a result of which the human is human only to the extent that he or she is a *homo narrantis* and *narratum*.[75] The three authors on storytelling to be considered here, in order to gauge what, from their perspective, has been done to those who can no longer speak about what they underwent in the camps, are Wilhelm Schapp, Walter Benjamin, and Hannah Arendt.[76] Each of these theories, none of which engages the questions I am pursuing here in any explicit or implicit way, are, first of all, very different theories as far as their conceptual frameworks are concerned. Schapp's theory concerning stories explicitly departs from the attitude predominant in the natural sciences in an attempt to solve the fundamental theme of all philosophy—that is, the origin of the world. The theory approaches this theme through the methods of description provided by classical phenomenological research focusing on the way the world is lived and experienced—that is, constituted by stories—rather than consisting of a material given independent of history that can be observed from the outside, objectively, and with the help of categories that conform to such a reality.[77] Benjamin's theory is framed by historico-theological concerns, and Arendt's account of stories and storytelling is an anthropo-political account. Needless to say, these frameworks—or, if you will, the broader narratives within which sense is made of stories—will have to be taken into consideration at the moment when the implications will be drawn about what it would mean to no longer be able to tell a story. But what all three of these theories have in common, although certainly not in the same way, not with the same degree of radicality, and not always with the desired consistency, is that stories are no longer understood as something that occurs from the outside to a stable and identical self, but are intrinsic to and formative of the self. A self is a self only insofar as it itself lives in stories or has a story for others. But the thus understood stories whose unity or synthesis make the self a self, do not form a unity of consciousness. It is a unity either on a supra-individual level, or bestowed by others on a self that is nothing but its stories, that is also only in the eyes of others, and primarily so only after the death of the self when its unfinished story is completed.

1

ENTANGLEMENT IN STORIES
(Wilhelm Schapp)

BENJAMIN'S AND ARENDT'S INFLUENTIAL ELABORATIONS ON storytelling are well known. However, this is not the case with Schapp, especially since none of his works have been translated into English and are not really known beyond the German-speaking world.[1] Hence, a short introduction may be warranted. Schapp studied law, but also philosophy in Freiburg under Heinrich Rickert and Georg Simmel. After becoming acquainted with Husserlian thought through Wilhelm Dilthey, he went to Göttingen where he studied with Edmund Husserl from 1905 to 1909. He was the second of Husserl's students to write a dissertation under his supervision. It was published in 1910 under the title *Beiträge zur Phänomenologie der Wahrnehmung* (*Contributions to the Phenomenology of Perception*). Despite being a work that both draws on and critically debates (though only implicitly so) Husserl's *Logical Investigations*, which had appeared ten years earlier and which, even later, remained Schapp's principal reference to phenomenology, his *Beiträge* are not simply a further development of phenomenological thought. The immediately striking features of this work are its almost complete lack of technical vocabulary, the radical refusal of all abstraction, the primary focus on sensible appearances and highly detailed descriptions of them, and, especially, its wholesale rejection of the idea of "general"—that is, eidetic objects. In other words, already in this early work Schapp departs from phenomenology as a philosophy of essences. Because of what Hermann Lübbe—in what is still one of the best discussions of Schapp's later work, *In Geschichten verstrickt*—has thus termed "the declared end of phenomenological Platonism, that is, of phenomenology as 'a philosophy of essence,'" Schapp's approach to perception has been qualified by some as an original phenomenological realism.[2] But Schapp's *Beiträge* also already prepared for the departure from classical phenomenology's understanding of perception as the prime experience, in which the encounter with what is given *in propria persona* takes place, to an experience of things exclusively within stories.[3] In any event, in order to achieve the objective of describing what happens in perception if it is to be the originary place of the encounter with the things themselves (*die Sachen selbst*), the *Beiträge* perform a radical, independent, uncompromising, even an idiosyncratic appropriation of the early concept (that is, before its transcendental turn) of phenomenological description. Applied to the phenomenon of sensible perception, Schapp executes this methodological program without recourse to concepts that he holds to be foreign to this phenomenon with the aim of raising "the logos of the sensible world" to consciousness as a *logos* thoroughly distinct from the concern with essences of pure thought.[4]

Thoroughly situated in the movement of phenomenological inquiry, Schapp's dissertation is, as I have already pointed out, not deferential to phenomenological thought as an academic discipline. It comes, therefore, as no surprise that he did not opt for a university career as a philosopher after having completed his dissertation. He pursued his training as a lawyer, which during his years in Göttingen already provided him with an independent income. Only after his retirement in the fifties of the past century, and the publication of numerous works on law-related matters, did Schapp return to his early interests. Incidentally, as he makes clear in his later books—particularly, in *In Geschichten verstrickt* (1953) and *Philosophie der Geschichten* (1959)—his primary concern in these works about stories and the philosophy of stories, which, as could be shown, continues his early phenomenological investigation into the *logos* of the aesthetic world, is fundamentally indebted to his practice as a jurist for whom each case is, indeed, a function of the stories that constitute it.[5] As we will see, stories, even as they represent for Schapp the most originary phenomena, are anything but eidetical forms. They are intrinsically concrete and tangible formations (*Gebilde*), not only in general but also for each singular individual entangled in them. In his exploration of the human being's entanglement in stories, Schapp undoubtedly has Husserl's concerns with the lifeworld in mind. But the first part of *In Geschichten verstrickt* is devoted to an analysis of the *Wozudinger*—that is, of things that are created by humans for a specific purpose—in the production of which, "world" emerges.[6] This analysis is a clear indication that Schapp's work is above all a response to Heidegger's analytic of Dasein in *Being and Time*, and more precisely, to the latter's analysis of equipment, or rather, of useful things (*Zeug*). By taking as his starting point the structures of the creation of *Wozudinger*, Schapp argues that rather than being a preexisting frame for such creation, the "world" is formed as the surrounding world by this creation so as to subsequently manifest itself in the stories in which the human being finds him- or herself entangled. In other words, the world is a moment in stories, intelligible only through the unity that characterizes them, and is equi-original with the creation of *Wozudinger*.

More generally speaking, *In Geschichten verstrickt* takes aim at Heidegger's reference in *Being and Time* to Plato's *Sophist* and his demand not to engage "in telling a story" about Being, and Dasein's way of being in the world.[7] In contrast, Schapp argues that the analysis of *Wozudinger* shows that all these things are woven into contexts, frames, or horizons, and that it is impossible to experience or account for them independently of these relations. The intended point of the analyses of these contexts or horizons within which the *Wozudinger* created by humans are embedded, and which correspond to what Schapp understands by stories, is to show that such analyses never result in the discovery of general concepts—of the order of genres or species, for example—that could serve to account for them in general or ultimately, by way of a concept such as Being, but only in more stories. Although Heidegger's name is not even once mentioned in the book, *In Geschichten verstrickt* seeks to counter Heidegger's existential understanding of Dasein's world in terms of the general question of the meaning of Being, holding that, in truth, the human being is, as the title suggests, entangled in stories, and that its world is one of stories. Stories, as Schapp understands them, are thus, as the reference to entanglement suggest, of the order of an existential condition of the human being, in advance of their potential linguistic articulation. Their being told is, as Paul Ricoeur remarks in a brief reference to Schapp in *Time and Narrative*, a "secondary process."[8] The very potentiality of a human being's story to be told is thus rooted in the stories in which such a being finds him- or herself existentially entangled from the start. Such entanglement is, as Schapp notes, characterized by "internal silent speech," which may be thought of as the mediating condition that makes it possible for the stories to be explicitly told.[9] Not all stories are necessarily told, but qua the silent speech that accompanies them, they are governed by the *telos* of being told. Actual realization in the form of a told story is grounded in the silent speech that accompanies it and that presses it to be told, to be communicated. In the second part of the book, entitled "*Verstricktsein in Geschichten und in Geschichte* [Entanglement in Stories and in History]," Schapp goes one step further: "The tradition considers stories and history to be something *in* the world. By contrast, for us, the world and history in which we are entangled are the same. For us the world is only in history, or, at first, only in the stories, in which the individual is entangled or co-entangled."[10] Rather than situating the human being within the perspective of the history of Being—a history in the singular—the human being's world, according to Schapp, is constituted by a plurality of histories or stories. Stories as told stories, but also history in the sense of *historia*, are verbal or literary formations that presuppose the human being's entanglement in a world of stories—including those of others, which in being told are spun further through their narration. As Schapp writes, the one reason for narrating stories in which one is entangled is not that they are finished and may be passed on, but they "are stories that [as living stories] are driven forward, that should continue, that is, stories in which the place from which one starts [*angegangene Stelle*] should write, as it were, the continuation."[11] Certainly at first, the notion of entanglement suggests the passivity of the one who finds him- or herself in the midst of a story. But stories are not finished end products. Indeed, the seeming passivity of the entangled one is counterbalanced by the telling and retelling of his or her story, which makes the story actively move forward.[12]

For Schapp, what is fundamental is not the problematic of Being. Stories, by contrast, are of primary significance, and from them alone, humans, animals, things emerge, entangled in them. Entanglement (*Verstrickung*, though at times he also speaks of *Verwicklung*) is the very way in which one or something *is*, and that means, is within a story. As already mentioned, Schapp systematically avoids philosophical terminology and categorization. Thus, rather than "being-in" (*In-Sein*) which according to Heidegger is a fundamental existential structure of Dasein regarding its relation to the world, the notion of entanglement (*Verstrickung*), taken from ordinary language, serves him to describe, in accordance certainly with what Husserl had called the "natural view of the world," one's living relation to it. In English as well as in German the term has mostly negative connotations of being ensnarled, embroiled, imprisoned, or caught in something that hampers or obstructs—a lie, or contradictions, for example.[13] In general the prefix *Ver-* serves to amplify the noun or verb that it precedes—as in the case of the noun *Verstrickung*, the state of being entangled—and such amplification potentially has a latent pejorative signification. But when it comes to being entangled in stories, "entanglement" has such negative connotations only if the stories that happen to a subject affect it from the outside, rather than from within.

Let us start out by noting that the primary meaning of the term "*Verstrickung*" refers to the operation of knitting, and it means to use or finish up the knitting yarn. As the prefix *Ver-* indicates, even in its figural sense of being entangled, "*Verstrickung*" designates the state of being within a knitted fabric and, in the case of Schapp's use of the term, being within the texture or web of a story. Indeed, the expression of being "*verstrickt*" literally suggests finding oneself in a fabric, or a web of narration. And by the same token, what one is entangled in—namely, stories—are therefore of the order of a web or woven pattern. Schapp points out that "he uses the expression 'entanglement' in a broad sense, and that he wishes the term 'the entangled one' to refer to anyone to whom a story happens, who stands in its middle, or belongs to it."[14] The term thus suggests that the human being is not first an independent entity to whom stories happen subsequently, but that he or she is from the start within stories and is what he or she is only by being entangled in stories. A story never happens to oneself from the outside. One is always within stories. Entanglement thus means involvement-in, and it suggests, in particular, that one can never extricate or abstract oneself from what is fundamental—namely, being in stories—precisely because such fundamental entanglement in stories is the condition for being what one is, a human being. Since entanglement is not something provoked by some stories and not by others, but rather is what makes the story a story to begin with, it is impossible to exit from it. But such entanglement does not signify a form of divine natural necessity as personified by *Ananke*, who spins the fate of gods and men on her adamantine spindle. In no way does it suggest a fatalist lack of freedom by the one involved in it, not only because one is what one is to the extent only that one has a story, but also because one has not just one story but stories in the plural. As the titles of his works indicate, entanglement is a *plurale tantum*. By its nature entanglement is an involvement in always multiple stories. Indeed, as Marquard points out, "only he who participates in many stories, has—by way of the separation of those powers that are the stories—through the one story a freedom from the respective other story. He or she who has only one story does not possess this freedom."[15] Since the entanglement Schapp has in mind is one in multiple stories, it is also a condition of the human being's freedom insofar as it frees him or her from a monolithic total and totalizing story.

A commentary on one passage in particular from *In Geschichten verstrickt* should help me bring into relief those characteristics of stories that in Schapp's work might be pertinent to what interests me in this study. Schapp remarks,

> [w]ith each story the one who is entangled in it or those who are entangled in it come into view (*tauchen auf*). The story stands for the man. It extends, or deepens itself without effort on our part, as it were, into the man depending on the weight inherent in the story. We also are of the opinion that the access to the man, to the human being, is accomplished only through stories, through only his stories, and that the corporeal appearance of the human being is also only an appearance of his stories; that his face, for example, also tells stories in its

own way, and that the body is a body for us only insofar as it tells stories or, and this amounts to the same, hides or seeks to hide stories.[16]

The sentences, which state that "a story stands for the man," or a few lines further, "that each story stands for a human being," condense in the most succinct fashion the fundamental signification that, according to Schapp, stories have for understanding the human being.[17] As he explains, "[W]ith this we mean that our ultimate (*letztmöglichen*) access to the human being is through the stories we have of him."[18] Hence the significance of all stories. Indeed,

> [w]hat we essentially know about human beings seems to be their stories and the stories that surround them. Through his story we encounter [*kommen wir in Berührung*, in tactile fashion, that is also, and at the same time, the happening of a becoming entangled through such touch in] another self. The human being is not the human being as a being of flesh and blood. In its place his story imposes itself on us as what is most proper to him (*sein Eigentliches*).[19]

At one point, stories are referred to as "the last intelligible part in itself of a non-closed whole that comes into view with it," and are, subsequently, compared to atoms.[20] "Entanglement is the final indivisible part," by means of which justice is to be done to what being human properly means.[21] What the human being is, in essence, in his or her very humanity, in what is most proper about him or her, in his or her very selfhood, is defined by his or her concrete stories, and tangibly accessible (in tactile fashion—that is, sensibly) only through these individual and singular stories in which he or she is entangled.

At this juncture the reason why I precede the discussion of storytelling in Benjamin and Arendt by extensively exploring Schapp's philosophy of stories should become clear. For what interests me in this study—the phenomenon of the inability of the survivors of the holocaust to tell their stories—it is Schapp who makes the most sweeping case for the fundamental role that stories and storytelling represent with respect to the human condition. From the perspective of Schapp's assessment, the muteness of the holocaust survivors appears literally as a *skandalon*—that is, both an annoyance or offence—to such a theory and a snare or trap into which it falls when venturing to address this phenomenon. For, indeed, as my conclusions suggest, the muteness in question is a trap that when addressed in theories about the story and storytelling, might force them to reconsider the nature of the story as a form of sense.

Stories, consequently, are the most primary as regards the nature of being human. According to its concept, a story implies that rather than being withheld, it is told to be heard. But before I pursue the importance of these implications, I must linger for a moment on the stories themselves. Each human being is entangled in many stories. After having evoked stories that are one's own (*Eigengeschichten*) and that, furthermore, weigh heavily on oneself (*die einem im Nacken sitzen*), Schapp writes that "[s]tories may remind one of scarred wounds, that at any time can reopen, or of wounds that do not heal at all."[22] Not all the stories in which one is involved are thus of the same order. Following these stories, with which one actively seeks to come to grips in one way or another, Schapp brings up "the flight or escape from one's particular stories," which he characterizes as a flight from the world (*Weltflucht*).[23] Needless to say, these stories from which one flees, are also stories that press hard, if not too hard, on oneself. But such flight or escape from stories, Schapp holds, "belongs also to the stories."[24] For Schapp then, one is never without a story; if by fleeing from one story, one still is within a story, this means that all flight from stories is a flight into another story. Now, as regards all those stories that press hard upon oneself, whether one tries to cope with them or flee from them, "the ultimate (*letzte*) stigma that characterizes them is that they are *my* stories."[25] These particular stories or stories that are my own (*Eigengeschichten*) are stigmata, not only in the sense of being marks that ultimately define oneself, but also in the sense that as marks burned into me, they resemble wounds like those of the crucified body of Christ. As such, these stories are my utmost own stories, the essential stories in which I am entangled and that say who, ultimately, I am. Insofar as they are mine, these stories "are separated as it were from the stories of others by a wall over which one cannot climb."[26] But in the same way as the stories in which others are entangled are the only way to come close to them, "our own stories— the way in which we live them (*wie wir sie bestehen*), and are entangled in them, the way they loosen or become inextricable," are the only way to come close to oneself.[27] But it is also always only from within the horizon of the stories in which one is entangled, and from whose story-world one cannot exit, that one can encounter oneself.[28]

As I have pointed out already, stories qua stories imply that they are told and addressed to those who listen to them. A singular story, Schapp writes, "is intended to be retold."[29] From this it follows that living stories (*lebendige Geschichten*) are never finished products; they continue by being retold. As a result, "each story stands in a living interconnectedness with other stories, perhaps, with all stories."[30] Schapp adds that "one can perhaps say that each story is prepared within the horizon of each other story, or that there is a place for the other stories within the horizon of each story."[31] In short, a story as a story is a told story; it is what it is only if it can be, and is, shared with others. Through their intrinsic communicability stories are never isolated stories—an isolated story is a contradiction in terms. They are never untold because they might be untellable. On the contrary, they are interconnected in a living, hence not closed, larger whole, in which what began with a story continues to have effects and consequences. For this reason, Schapp could also contend that the flight from one's utmost own story still belongs to one's story.

The problematic I am interested in requires the examination of still one more aspect of Schapp's theory of stories. In order to further develop the role played by the one who is entangled in a story, Schapp makes a distinction between self-entanglement (*Selbstverstrickung*) and the entanglement of an other in a story (*Fremdverstrickung*). One's belonging to a story always appears to a listener, reader, or judge as an entanglement of an other in a story. If Schapp considers self-entanglement to be "the core of his study," is it not because, thanks to a story's intrinsic appeal to listeners, this entanglement also concerns the inevitable perception or experience of the self by an other self?[32] All entanglement of an other is, Schapp states, "the self-entanglement of an other," the implication being that entanglement in stories is the fundamental mode in which the selfhood of others is experienced.[33] Without another's self-entanglement in a story, no access whatsoever to him- or herself is possible. More precisely, such self-entanglement is not only the condition of selfhood but also of all possible relations between the self and others. But what about the relation of this self to others who encounter it through its stories, and who themselves are what they are only insofar as they live in their own stories? How does "the self-entanglement of an other relate to my own entanglement?" Schapp asks.[34] The question concerns the relation, or participation of "the most proper," or "utmost own [*eigensten*] story" of each singular human being—his or her "*ureigene Geschichte*"—in the stories of others.[35] According to Schapp, the lines of connections, the interconnections between stories regarding the self, oneself, and the stories of others point to an ultimate commonality (*Gemeinsamkeit*) that concerns being human itself. According to Schapp, "being human is exhaustively determined by this entanglement in stories: the human being is the one who is entangled in stories."[36] In other words, being human not only means to have a story of one's own, but to have a story that is entangled in the stories of others and vice-versa. This web-like entanglement constitutes and is the ultimate commonality of being human.

Before I pose the question regarding the consequences that, according to Schapp, would follow from the destruction of one's ability to tell one's story, it must be pointed out that in *Philosophie der Geschichten*, Schapp acknowledges the fact that one can be ordered to hold one's tongue. But a prohibition to speak, to speak aloud, does not affect what he termed "silent speech," which continues to accompany the stories that press hard to be told.[37] Though forbidden to tell one's story, both the ability to silently speak and the power to loudly speak remain intact. A prohibition to speak in no way impairs one's capacity to do so. Yet such impairment of the ability to speak both aloud and silently is what is at issue with the soldiers returning from World War I and, in particular, with holocaust survivors.

Stories, Schapp holds, are wholes, totalities, and are constantly present as such wholes or totalities in the course they take.[38] The past and the future always belong in an original fashion to the whole they represent. In addition, the stories themselves, as such wholes, have a beginning and end that are grounded in what precedes and follows them. Only in being interconnected in this fashion to stories that precede and follow them do they possess unity and wholeness. But if this is so, can an inmate of a death camp have a story at all? If in the world of the inmates there is only "stagnant time," and "history has stopped," as Levi reports, this world no longer has the temporal unity of stories.[39] It lacks the web-like structure in which humans qua humans are entangled. Cut off from their past and being exposed to a future that is no longer a future since it means certain death—which as Levi has noted, is, in the case of the Muselmänner (most of whom, significantly, were Jews), no longer a death properly speaking, and, I add, no longer experiencable in a succession of events—the inmates cannot even be said to have had a present.[40] For them the in-between in which life unfolds, constituted by a beginning and an end, no longer obtains. Furthermore, narrating one's story presupposes a sequential order, an interlocking sequencing of events; but if time has become stagnant, it is no longer possible to link occurrences into an unfolding course of events. Yet if already for temporal reasons alone the lives of the inmates of the death camps can no longer take on the form of a story, they also are no longer entangled. The existential category of entanglement no longer seems to make any sense in their case. Entanglement in stories is constitutive of the singularity of an individual, a singularity of which the inmates have been stripped at the very moment a number has been tattooed into their flesh. In distinction from the story that is one's own—mine—and that like a stigma says who I am, the number engraved in one's flesh deprives one immediately of a story of one's own. It makes one storyless. The number spells what I am for the oppressor, not for me, nor for others for whom my story is the only way to encounter me in a sensible and tactile fashion in all of my singularity. And since the story that the number in one's flesh tells is not my story, but who, or rather *what* I am for the oppressive other, the camp inmate has no story anymore and thus evidently has nothing to tell. His or her muteness is not deliberate; it results from the dispossession of a story of his or her own.

But could one not also hold that the survivor has only one single story, a *Sondergeschichte* as it were, one that allows for no other stories beside it—that is, a story that lifts the subject from its entanglement in multiple stories? Preventing the subject from having other stories, such a dominating story forced upon the victim is one that, in Schapp's understanding of being entangled, deprives the subject of all freedom and turns entanglement into a nightmarish hell. The inability to tell one's story would thus imply that at the limit one has no story anymore because having only one story equals having none, and that, as a consequence, one thus lacks all possible singularity. Because they are untellable, the untold stories of the holocaust survivors do not let themselves become part of the region and regimen of stories—of what Schapp called the "ultimate commonality of human beings' entanglement in stories." If, furthermore, all stories somehow fit themselves, as Schapp asserts, "into the grand stories-reality [*Geschichten-Wirklichkeit*] (if we are allowed to speak of such a thing), and participate in it," it also follows that the untold stories of the holocaust survivors and, by the same token, the individual's inability to forge a singularity, are excluded from that reality.[41] In short, the muted victims fall entirely outside of "the grand-stories reality," history tout court. Having no story, they also have no history that would embed them in a "grand stories-reality."

From what we have seen so far, having no story to tell affects both the very identity of the self and its participation in the web created by the ultimate commonality of being human—that is, in this web in its synchronic and diachronic dimensions. A self dispossessed of the ability in question would be lacking a self and a world: in short, such a self would, according to Schapp, necessarily fall entirely outside the network of stories in which human beings are entangled and co-entangled. Such a self would be an abstraction impossible to comprehend except as an abstraction, with which one could not come into tangible contact. This raises an additional question. In a discussion of the issue of "mutual understanding [*Verständigung*]," and its presupposition of being entangled in a story common to all, Schapp points out that "what is important about mutual understanding is not that one understands the other, but that the miracle of [understanding] already presupposes the possibility of reception, and the readiness of reception of the whole human being together with his whole story within humanity with its [whole] story."[42] In sum, the inability to tell stories does not only prevent inter-human understanding; on a deeper level it is a sign of the breakdown of the miracle of understanding—that is, of reception as the very condition of the possibility of mutual understanding, a breakdown of which no possible story could tell the story. However, such a breakdown is something that Schapp's theory of storytelling can in no way envision—what he advances about the flight or escape from one's story still takes place within a story—since it does not occur within a story to begin with. On the basis of the fundamental tenets of Schapp's theory on stories, the breakdown referred to is a *skandalon*. As already suggested, the silent speech that accompanies all stories, and that predisposes them to be told, is the condition of possibility for assuming the form that makes stories communicable. But the muteness that one encounters with the survivors of the extermination camps, if it is not simply a silence about what they have endured, implies the silencing of the silent speech that imbues stories with an inclination toward being told, and that makes their telling into the constituting goal of what a story is. In short, if this silent speech has been silenced the victim cannot possibly have a story. Yet, within Schapp's theory such a thing seems to be unthinkable. If the story of having no story is not an issue, it is because such a non-story cannot be told. To explicitly acknowledge such a possibility would require rethinking what a story is.

There is no place in Schapp's theory for considering the possibility of a full destruction of what Benjamin called an "inalienable possession," which in fact, had so far been considered the securest of all our possessions. If at all conceivable such a possibility can, for Schapp, at best be considered only in the abstract, as an inconsequential play on words, a non sequitur. But perhaps Schapp faces the possibility of the scandalous nonetheless in the form of a more menacing form of abstraction. To substantiate this suggestion, I briefly turn to his *Philosophie der Geschichten*, where, interestingly enough, it is pointed out that "stories are ur-phenomena, ur-formations, much more originary [*urhafter*] than the formations of science."[43] Stories, then, compete with the formations of the sciences. Given the ur-phenomenal nature of stories, the inability to tell stories reflecting the human being's existential condition of being entangled in stories is a clear indication that the depletion of this ability would radically strip a human being of his or her humanity. Yet indeed, such a possibility materializes in Schapp's reflections in the context of what the sciences do with their formations to the human being: they reduce the world and the human being to abstractions that have no existence, abstractions that deplete the human being of his or her constituting ability to form and live in stories. "Abstraction," in Schapp's work, I suggest, is the formation within which the problematic of the complete divestment of stories is indirectly envisaged, and at the same time completely covered over. Schapp's entire theory of stories is geared as a response to this dehumanizing threat that, according to him, lurks in the formations of scientific (and philosophical) abstractions. Indeed, the frame within which Schapp takes up the issue of stories is motivated by the Husserlian device or motto: "To the things themselves," which he, however, understands as those of the real and sensible world in which there are, in distinction from the philosophical or scientific world, no such abstractions. But by opposing the concreteness of stories to the so-called abstractions of sciences, does Schapp relieve himself of the means of thinking not only what threatens the story from within, but also what it is that makes them tellable to begin with?

2

STORYTELLING
(Walter Benjamin)

THE STORY OF A LOST ARTISANAL WORLD TAKES CENTER STAGE within the historico-theological context that frames Benjamin's development of his theory of stories and storytelling. As we see in due time, stories are crafted artifacts and the storyteller a craftsman.[1] Both presuppose a world of artisanal modes of production in which stories are woven, not unlike the products of the craft of spinning and weaving—activities that Benjamin singularly highlights as lending themselves, because of the mechanical nature of the work they demand, in exemplary fashion to telling and, in particular, listening to stories. It is a kind of work that creates self-forgetfulness on the part of the workers, which in turn makes them capable of listening. But these two crafts, spinning and weaving, are not just mentioned in passing by Benjamin as we see in a moment. In any event, with the industrialization of work, this world of the artisan and the work that produces avid listeners of stories has disappeared. This decline of storytelling occurs through a temporal succession of events that follow upon one another, and that itself has the form of story authorized by the death of storytelling, which endows it with the unity that a story qua story must possess. Let me evoke only those aspects of the story in question that are pertinent to the overall problematic I am concerned with here—that is, the inability of the returning soldiers of

World War I, and especially the survivors of the death camps in World War II, to tell their stories.

Benjamin's theory of stories and storytelling, rather than simply being a discursive account of this subject matter, takes the form of a story of its own—a story explicitly linked to the question of time. For instance, the loss of the art of storytelling is explained by a contemporary person's lack of time for having experiences. However, before anything else, the reasons for this decline of storytelling need to be worked out. What Benjamin says about the soldiers returning from the battlefield muted concerns a process that only with the end of World War I became manifest (*offenkundig*), and which, hence, is no longer possible to ignore. Not only has this process not halted since then, it has also, as Benjamin indicates, been underway for a long time. The "earliest foreboding [*Anzeichen*]" of this "process whose end is the decline of storytelling is the rise of the novel at the beginning of modern times," Benjamin remarks. Yet what thus comes to an end with the rise of the novel is, precisely, a process that has not only been going on for a long time (as the English translator says), but that also "comes from far away [*von weither kommt*]."[2] Indeed, even though the novel arises only in modernity, "its beginnings go back to antiquity," to the genre of the satire, to be precise.[3] But, by speaking of the process in question as one that comes from far away, Benjamin also suggests that it originates much earlier than in antiquity. Indeed, in order to fully gauge what exactly, according to Benjamin, is lost with the art of storytelling, it is necessary to reach back to the origin of this process in what I term an "immemorial (*unvordenkliche*) past." It is a process that not only comes from far away, which has been long in the making, but which also evolves at a such a slow pace that it has been imperceptible until the first signs of it made it fully manifest and impossible to ignore. Benjamin writes: "One must imagine the transformation of epic forms occurring in rhythms comparable to those of the change that has come over the earth's surface in the course of thousands of centuries. Hardly any other forms of human communication have taken shape more slowly, been lost more slowly."[4] The comparison of the decline of the epic art with geological transformations of the surface of the earth—a comparison intended to highlight the long, slow, and imperceptible process of the loss in question—is not only part and parcel of Benjamin's imagery in "The Storyteller," but also of the story within which the decline of storytelling is narrated. Benjamin continues:

> It took the novel, whose beginnings go back to antiquity, hundreds of years before it encountered in the evolving middle class those elements that were favorable to its flowering. With the appearance of these elements, storytelling began to recede very gradually into the archaic. True, in many ways it took hold of the new material but was not really determined by it.[5]

The "elements" that appeared with the burgeoning bourgeois class concern the profound isolation of the bourgeois individual, his or her inability to make sense of the world, and signals what Lukacs, in *The Theory of the Novel*, calls the individual's "transcendental homelessness."[6] Yet, even though Benjamin explicitly refers to the individual's homelessness, according to him, this is not the material that determines the flowering of the novel. On the contrary, what determines it is something much older than the epic, much older than narration: something archaic that affects the narration involved in the novel to such a degree so as to determine the latter's essence. This archaic state into which storytelling gradually recedes is something from which storytelling had egressed, or from which it had liberated itself in immemorial times, but into which it now seems to fatally recede. Based on what we have seen so far regarding the soldiers' returning mute and muted from the battlefield, unable to tell what they experienced, the order of this archaic state is, inexorably, one of muteness. This archaic muteness—which Benjamin attributes elsewhere to the human being's entanglement in myth—from which storytelling emerged by breaking with it, has threatened storytelling ever since, throughout the slow and imperceptible yet steady process of its deterioration, which finally became manifest in the muteness of the soldiers returning from the battlefield. But in analyzing the forces that threaten storytelling today, Benjamin not only limits himself to the threat that comes from afar, from a mythic immemorial past, but also conceives of this threat as one that is caused by forces originating in the present, if not even in the future. Discussing the threat to whatever remains of storytelling in the novel, information is shown to play a possibly even more menacing role than the danger that looms over it from the past. Storytelling thus appears squeezed to extinction between, on the one hand, the return of the forces of archaic muteness and, on the other, blaring information, which, at first, seems to be its opposite, but whose short-lived and superficial quality of unending babble shows it to be a force not unrelated to that of archaic times.

At this junction it is imperative to get a better grasp of Benjamin's understanding of what storytelling consists of and what it accomplishes. The end of the art of storytelling is said to correspond to the loss of a possession of "something that seemed inalienable to us"—namely, "the ability to exchange experiences."[7] The muteness that has replaced storytelling is a symptom of a decline of experience, since experience is something that by its very nature is always "passed on from mouth to mouth," thus something essentially communicable and which, if it is not told or is prevented from being told, is no longer an experience to begin with.[8] This fundamental link between experience and communication is indicative of the fact that experience (unlike *Erlebnisse*) is not something that is simply private or personal. Experience has, from the beginning, the structure of a story and is thus directed to others with whom it is exchanged. The loss of the art of storytelling is testimony, therefore, not only to the fact that experiences are no longer made, but also to the disintegration of the fabric of human interrelations that it presupposes and fosters. The loss of storytelling reflects a complete isolation of the individual human being. But what is it exactly that occurs in storytelling that it should fundamentally shape human interrelations through its communication of experiences? As Benjamin submits, "[a]n orientation toward practical interests is characteristic of many born storytellers."[9] This feature, he continues, points to the very nature of "every real [*wahren*] story"—that is, every story that is truly a story. Any real story "contains, openly or covertly, something useful. In one case, the usefulness may lie in a moral; in another, in some practical advice; in a third, in a proverb or maxim. In every case the storyteller is a man who has counsel for his readers."[10] In storytelling, then, the experiences that are communicated give counsel to the listeners who, qua listeners of stories, are interested in getting practical advice in, at first, a broad sense. But it is in a narrower, and at the same time, in a more essential sense that having counsel determines Benjamin's understanding of the role of storytelling in human life. In any case, having counsel (*Rat wissen*) is what characterizes a storyteller; and, as the communication of experiences, true stories, by definition, give counsel. If this notion of the ability of having or giving counsel, or the lack thereof of the modern individual—who, because of the decrease of the communicability of experience, has neither counsel for him- or herself nor for others—underlies Benjamin's whole analysis of storytelling, it has to be looked at more carefully if we are to elicit the consequences of the disappearance of this seemingly inalienable possession of the human being.

First, however, it may be appropriate to return to the question of information, which, apart from the archaic forces, endangers storytelling in the present day. Information, Benjamin explains, supplies its recipient with "a handle (*Anhaltspunkt*) for what is nearest"—in other words, with clues about how to go about things that happen within one's immediate proximity.[11] Providing a handle, however, is not the same as giving counsel. On the contrary! In addition to its timed utility and its short life, the handle offered by information is grounded in the latter's prompt verifiability and plausibility. Distinct from "intelligence [*Kunde*] coming from afar" (whether in a spatial or temporal sense), which is communicated through stories, information, for Benjamin, possesses no authority, and hence "proves incompatible with the spirit of storytelling."[12] Whereas stories are not per se plausible because they are "inclined to borrow from the miraculous," and especially because of a certain perplexity intrinsic to them, which is instrumental to their reception, information, in order to provide handles, "must appear 'understandable in itself.'"[13] It must offer itself from the start as a patent means to address issues that are of an immediate concern. The validity of information thus resides in itself and is independent from any relation to another person. Its origin is the radio or the press. Stories, by contrast, in spite of their lack of plausibility, derive their significance for a listener from another human being, more precisely, the storyteller, a person endowed with authority. The implausibility of stories allows them to arrive to their readers (*uns ... erreicht*) in the first place and to touch them with their perplexity, causing the readers or listeners to reflect, thus making the stories work for them. As a consequence, an intrinsic net of social relations is at play in storytelling. For the story to provide counsel, it must contain something implausible that the storyteller must authoritatively vouch for, which, in turn, draws the listeners to it, allowing them to appropriate it over time through an interpretation that allows the story to impress itself upon them. Such a net of intra-human relations is no longer present with information, which is plausible in itself, comes from one source that does not imply direct human contact, and is passively received by the recipient.

Let me return to the issue of the counsel that stories have for an other human being. Following his statement that because of the decrease of communicable experiences we no longer have counsel either for ourselves or for others, Benjamin muses:

> After all, counsel is less an answer to a question than a proposal concerning the continuation of a story which is in the process of unfolding. To seek this counsel one would first have to be able to tell the story (Quite apart from the fact that a man is receptive to counsel only to the extent that he allows his situation to speak).[14]

The counsel that a story has for a listener, which unlike information is not a response to a question of how to handle a critical situation, concerns the story in which this listener finds him- herself, and is thus a proposal of how to continue the story in which he finds himself, a story that therefore concerns not a fleeting moment but her whole life. The counsel that stories provide presupposes that a hearer is immersed in an unfolding story and that the hearer seeks counsel of what direction to take for its continuation. Consequently, the counsel that defines stories is not simply any counsel in a broad sense, but it specifically concerns options regarding how to continue the story in which one is already involved. Needless to say, one has to be able to tell one's story in order to receive advice in the first place. In distinction from Schapp—for whom entanglement in stories is an irrepressibly essential, permanent, and immutable condition that constitutes the human being, to the point that even flight from stories signifies being in stories—for Benjamin having a story, or stories, and hence being woven into a social fabric of exchange of experiences, has, on the contrary, become a highly fragile condition.[15] The seemingly inalienable possession of stories and storytelling is, then, in fact a highly precarious one. Or, differently put, what happened to storytelling in the present is a sign that it never has been an inalienable possession of the human. As the historical development from archaic times to the present recession demonstrates, it is a condition constantly menaced by extinction. The experiences on which stories rest, and thus their communicability, are in an accelerating process of disappearing. But, here, in the lines just quoted, Benjamin concedes also that stories can have counsel only for those who "allow [their] situation to speak"—in other words, for those who are capable of telling their story—thus acknowledging the very possibilities of both refusing and of not being able to do so, and consequently of having ultimately no story, no communicable experience, which, as we have seen, ultimately amounts to no longer being human, no longer being embedded in a web of human relations.

In "The Storyteller," Benjamin retraces the long process of the decline of storytelling back to the archaic and to myth. But he also reaches back through the literary genre of the novel, not only to the form of the epic and the form of the story properly speaking, but to the story's earliest form—that is, the fairy tale. After the assertion that all great storytellers have their roots in the people, and that the experience that finds expression in their stories is a collective rather than an individual experience, Benjamin evokes the ease (*Unbeschwertheit*) with which the storytellers

> move up and down the rungs of their experience, as if on a ladder. A ladder extending downward to the interior of the earth and disappearing in the clouds: this is the image for a collective experience to which even the deepest shock in every individual experience—death—constitutes no impediment or barrier.[16]

Comparing a ladder to the ease with which a storyteller rooted in a collective experience delves into extremes such as the inanimate and the animate, Benjamin not only refers to a frequent motive of fairy tales, but also establishes the rootedness of the form of stories in the popular genre of the fairy tale itself. He writes:

> The fairy tale, which to this day is the first tutor of children because it was once the first tutor of mankind, secretly lives on in the story. The first true storyteller is, and will continue to be, the teller of fairy tales. Whenever good counsel was at a premium, the fairy tale had it, and where the need was greatest, its aid was nearest. This need was the need created by myth. The fairy tale tells us of the earliest arrangements that mankind made to shake off the nightmare which myth had placed upon its chest.[17]

With this passage the larger historico-theological framework of Benjamin's theory of storytelling becomes tangible. Every constitutive aspect of a story, as Benjamin sees it, draws its significance from this framework, which therefore needs to be deployed in greater detail before the implications of Benjamin's theory can fully come into relief. The fairy tale is the first tutor of humankind. From archaic times, when human beings where enmeshed in a world interconnecting guilt and fate, the fairy tale provided counsel on how to free oneself from the powers of myth. It is here that one can gauge the full importance that giving counsel has for Benjamin's understanding of the nature of the story. Counsel is, ultimately, what makes it possible to break from the entanglement of myth and its nightmares, which prevent humans from having a story to begin with, a story that, thanks to the council of the storyteller, can be carried on, that can have a *Fortsetzung*—that is, a "to follow"—not unlike the announcement at the end of stories published in journals that there will be a continuation. It is this advice that the fairy tale has for how to break with myth, which secretly lives on in the counsel that all stories, thereafter, have been able to dispense. Older than the epic, the fairy tale, by communicating a way out of myth, goes back to the state of humankind following the Fall. The arrangement that it provides for humanity to shake off the powers of myth and of post-lapsarian nature is contemporaneous with the Fall itself. Now, interestingly enough, Benjamin links the contemporaneity of the fairy tales' answer to the nightmare that myth placed on the chest of humankind to Origines's doctrine of *apokatastasis*. This doctrine plays a significant role throughout "The Storyteller" even though it is mentioned only toward its end. The Christian theologian's doctrine of *apokatastasis* refers to the universal restoration of all to God, establishing that everyone without exception will be saved in the end and enter paradise. Benjamin evokes Origines's doctrine in the context of his characterization of Nikolai Leskov as one of the very few storytellers "who have so profound a kinship with the spirit of the fairy tale."[18] The fact that Leskov might have been influenced by this doctrine is not so surprising after all, since it is a doctrine that has been promoted by the Greek Orthodox Church. More surprising, by contrast, is the implicit assertion of an intrinsic link between the fairy tale and the doctrine in question. So what is the relation of the fairy tale to Orgines's doctrine of *apokatastasis*? They are similar in spirit, Benjamin suggests, because both consider the state of the world with which they are concerned to be an enchanted world (*verzaubert*), a world under a spell. But even more fundamental is the fact that Origines's heretic speculation provides the ultimate foundation and justification for the fairy tale's practical lessons on how to circumvent an enchanted world in which a spell has been cast on the living.[19] Indeed, only if everyone will in the end be redeemed is it possible to effectively break with the powers of myth in the first place by offering counsel, and therein to secure a story for human beings that can be continued, or carried on.

In the world of the fairy tale in which a spell has been cast on both animate and inanimate nature, the tales offer a way to break away from the forces of "mythical primordial time."[20] As all the examples that Benjamin gives demonstrate, the counsel offered by tales consists of how "to meet the forces of the mythical world with cunning and with excessive courage," with *List* and *Übermut*, which I translate, in turn, back into Greek, with *metis* and *hubris*.[21] In one of his examples, Benjamin evokes animals that come to the rescue of a child. This example shows that "nature not only is subservient to myth, but much prefers to be aligned with man."[22] Animate nature under the spell of the primordial forces of myth, however far its fall might be, and however much it is stricken with muteness, would prefer to be liberated from the forces that imprison it and can therefore be enlisted in the struggle of those to rise above the forces in question, ripping apart the tight web of entanglement in which they are held captive. But as Leskov's stories make explicit, in the story entitled "The Alexandrite" in particular, inanimate nature too is in complicity with humanity. Indeed, "the scale of created things" reaches down into the inanimate, and because it has been created, this domain also longs for liberation from the powers of myth. Although the complicity of the inanimate is a dominant motive in oral and anonymous storytelling before all writing, Leskov, according to Benjamin, is one of the very few modern storytellers to have ventured into the depths of the domain in question and, in the same breath, to have reconnected with the origins of storytelling itself. What is important about "The Alexandrite," which "deals with a semiprecious stone, the chrysoberyl," is that a "mineral [which] is the lowest stratum of created things," is "directly linked to the highest." Indeed, in this tale the stone in question, when cut, reveals to the gem cutter "a natural prophecy of petrified, lifeless nature—a prophecy that applies to the historical world in which he himself lives," and that concerns the fate of Alexander II—namely, the latter's premature death.[23] Through his analysis of Leskov's tale, Benjamin submits that stories not only offer council to the human being in a world subservient to the powers of mythical fate, but that everything in this world, from the animate to the inanimate, contains qua created things, itself a message to the living in the grip of archaic powers. In other words, stories, and more fundamentally, everything of the fairy tales that lives on in them, interlink the whole world from its lowest to its highest strata in a concerted attempt to end the muteness of the archaic. Being able to tell a story thus implies making all things, even those that are petrified—such as things of inanimate nature, or subservient to myth, as is the case with animals—speak, and speak both to the narrator and the hearer of the story. They give counsel, and this counsel derives its authority primarily from these things' creatural nature—that is, from the divine spark that, by virtue of having been created, animates even the inanimate. Because they are created, all creatures are allied with human beings against the demonic powers of myth.

Now that an outline, however succinct, of the historico-theological framework within which Benjamin's theory of storytelling unfolds is in place—a theory that contrasts with that of the narrative of the novel, which because of the latter's essential dependence on the book, is no longer indebted to the living voice and the creative nature of the divine *verbum*, and, a fortiori, to the oral tradition—we can return in somewhat greater detail to what Benjamin advances about the social network within which the telling of and listening to stories occurs, and, especially, about how storytelling contributes to, or rather constitutes, such social interconnectedness. When he holds that stories give counsel regarding how to continue a story in the process of unfolding, and that in order to seek such council one has to first, of course, be able to tell one's story, several things need to be highlighted. If, as Benjamin submits, "[c]ounsel is woven into the fabric

[*Stoff*] of real life (*gelebten Lebens*)," and that counsel by way of a story, rather than being an answer to a question, is a proposal for how to continue a currently unfolding story, then it is clear that "real life" consists in living in stories, and that its fabric is made up by the dialogical relationship between speakers and listeners.[24] In the fabric of real life, speakers, while letting their situation speak, listen to a storyteller who first listened to them so as to subsequently be able to tell a story that will have the potential of providing counsel to that other on how to carry on with their stories. If real life, "lived life," in short, is made up of a fabric or a web of stories that themselves interact with one another, on the one hand, by being told, listened to, and retold, and, on the other hand, by providing counsel for the continuation and extension of other stories, it is, first of all, because it is such a life in which people are allowed to let their situation speak—speaking consisting of narrating—so as to motivate an other (without explicitly asking for counsel) to tell a story that might be significant for the progression of the weaving of one's own story. This fabric of social life is one of an intricate exposure of listeners to storytellers, and vice-versa—a fabric that mutually binds them. This social fabric, which Benjamin finds fully realized in the world of craftsmanship, is "the web in which the gift of storytelling is cradled."[25] This reference by which storytelling is said to originate in the world of craftsmanship clearly demonstrates that the earlier talk about weaving and spinning as activities beneficial for the craft of storytelling was not accidental. As a craft, the activity of storytelling is itself a sort of spinning and weaving (even though Benjamin also uses other images to account for the craftsmanship of storytelling). Furthermore, lived life has a web-like structure in which actor and storyteller are inextricably interwoven. Weaving a life and listening to the counsel of the storyteller belong together. The two activities call upon one another and interlace in a weave-like warp that fills to form a web, the web of the social fabric.[26]

Of the storyteller, Benjamin writes that he "takes what he tells from experience—his own or that reported by others. And he in turn makes it the experience of those who are listening to his tale."[27] Stories, Benjamin avers, are crafted through patient work, involving an inordinate amount of time, in a way similar to the long processes evoked by Paul Valéry, in which nature creates small wonders such as "flawless pearls, full-bodied mature wines, truly developed [*wirklich durchgebildeten*] creatures."[28] As a craft, storytelling is still in harmonious sync with nature's long cycles of time. At one point, their formation is described in Benjamin's essay as consisting of the placing, or "slow[ly] piling up, one on top of the other, of thin, transparent layers," including "the layers of various retellings."[29] In conformity with Benjamin's consistent recourse to geological imagery in "The Storyteller," perfect stories have a micaceous structure of superposed transparent laminae. Those layers also render invisible the enormous amount of time that has gone into their fabrication, which not only likens stories to natural creations, but also frustrates all scientific attempts to render visible the work involved in them. Wherever it happens that the work that has gone into the creation of a story is fully exposed, the stories lose their quality of triggering the astonishment and, as a result, the reflection necessary for them to offer potential advice. In the context of his argument that stories resist explanation (such as psychological unfoldings could provide), Benjamin characterizes stories as perfect miniatures in terms of their "chaste compactness [*keusche Gedrungenheit*]."[30] Stories are stocky or squatty formations chastely holding to themselves. To explain their chaste compactness amounts to a rape. Now this very compactness of the story is what commits it to memory. The more a story resists explanation by way of its compactness, "the greater becomes the story's claim to a place in the memory of the listener; the more completely the story is integrated into the latter's own experience, the greater will be his inclination to repeat it to someone else someday, sooner or later."[31]

Telling a story that can be retold thus requires not only the skills of a craftsman, but also time, an amount of time requiring patience, which Benjamin associates with the extended cycles of natural time. To better understand what crafting a story that can be told and retold implies, and especially what the consequences would be of no longer being able to tell a story based on one's own experiences, at least a brief account of Benjamin's view of the temporality involved in stories and storytelling must be given. In analyzing the decline of the art of storytelling, Benjamin invokes Paul Valéry's observation that "[it] is almost as if the decline of the idea of eternity coincided with the increasing aversion to sustained effort," adding:

> The idea of eternity, that is, of timeless presence, has always had its strongest source in death. If this idea declines, so we reason, the face of death must have changed. It turns out that this change is identical with another—the one that has diminished the communicability of experience to the same extent as the art of storytelling has declined.[32]

The idea of eternity is introduced in the context of a description of the sphere of craftsmanship in which a person "works at what cannot be abbreviated," and, hence, "in which time did not matter."[33] However, how is one to understand Benjamin's somewhat enigmatic remark that "[t]he idea of eternity has always had its strongest source in death"? Is the answer simply that in a theologico-eschatological account of history, such as the one by which the chronicler as a history-teller accounts for the course of the world, the soul is held to be immortal and to live on in all eternity? Or, rather, is the answer to this question not to be found in what Benjamin advances about the efforts of the storyteller, who in contrast to the history-teller, makes the world's events intelligible by way of natural history?

Before deciding, let us first look at Benjamin's observations on how death was experienced in the artisanal and preindustrial world. Whereas in the general consciousness of modern people the omnipresence and vividness of death has dwindled, since "dying has been pushed further and further out of the perceptual world of the living" with the result that death is no longer experienced—an observation which makes Benjamin refer to modern people as "dry dwellers of eternity [*Trockenwohner der Ewigkeit*]"—"[d]ying was once a public process in the life of the individual and a most exemplary one."[34] Indeed, if life is the stuff stories are made of, death rounds them out and gives them authority, which, in turn, bestows authority on the storyteller who passes them on. In Benjamin's words:

> [C]haracteristically, it is not only a man's knowledge or wisdom, but above all his real life—and this is the stuff that stories are made of—which first assumes transmissible [*tradierbare*] form at the moment of his death. Just as a sequence of images is set into motion inside a man as his life comes to an end—unfolding the views of himself in which he has encountered himself without being aware of it—suddenly in his expressions and looks the unforgettable emerges, and imparts to everything that concerned him that authority which even the poorest wretch in the act of dying possesses for the living around him. This authority lies at the very origin of the story.[35]

Let us reemphasize that "[d]ying was once a public process in the life of the individual and a most exemplary one." To this, Benjamin adds: "[T]hink of the medieval pictures in which the deathbed has turned into a throne that people come toward through the wide-open doors of the dying person's house."[36] In other words, by reminding us of the way death is experienced in traditional preindustrial societies, Benjamin highlights its public nature. It is not a private moment. On the contrary, the departure of the living is a public event, and in a way an event that crowns their life. If transmissibility, and thus public passing on of a human being's knowledge or wisdom—that is, counsel for those left behind—takes place at precisely this moment of death, it is because at that moment the unforgettable part of one's story emerges for all to see. The unforgettable, revealed by a dying person's expression, not only brings the story of the deceased to a closure, but imparts on this story an authority regarding the living, entrusting it to collective memory. A whole life transfigured by the unforgettable that emerges with death takes on at that decisive moment the form of a story—in other words, accomplishes a level of ideality whose form makes it transmissible—and by the same token becomes immortal, or eternal, however finite or profane such eternality may be. If I speak of the *form* of the story as that which makes a life transmissible, it is not just a circumstantial expression. The unforgettable, or that which begs to be remembered and which is entrusted to memory, not only renders a life whole, it also provides it with an ideality that makes it repeatable, or transmissible. Memory accomplishes this through the form of a story.[37] Becoming a story at the hands of *Mnemosyne* is that by and toward which a real life, according to Benjamin, is oriented from the start, but which it accomplishes only at the moment of death when the unforgettable that characterizes a singular life is revealed to the dying and to those who experience that death, as a result of which a whole life is passed on as a story.[38] A story, then, is not simply an external recording of the facts of a life. It does not have any informational value. Through the unforgettable—that is, the irreducible singularity that elevates a real life to a story, that endows it with a transmissible form, and that gives it the authority it has—a story is what the dying pass on to the collectivity of those left behind. Being retold, the story continues to engage them; through the story the dead person remains involved with others.

What is crucial here is that at the moment of death, when a whole life acquires a form by which it can be passed on—namely, that of an authoritative story to be told—the temporality characteristic of that whole life has been that of natural time. Within the historico-theological framework of Benjamin's study of storytelling, what does this specific kind of time consist of? The unforgettable of a singular life, which comes into view at the moment of death, imparts a form and an authority on whatever can be told of the life in question. Benjamin avers: "Death is the sanction for everything that the storyteller can tell. He has borrowed his authority from death. In other words, his stories refer back to natural history."[39] Natural history, as opposed to that of salvation, acknowledges death in all its authority. Furthermore, the temporality characteristic of natural history itself is contingent upon the event of death. In the process of an analysis of a story by Hebel, Benjamin observes that natural history is one in which "[d]eath appears [...] with the same regularity as that of the Reaper in the processions that pass round the cathedral clock at noon."[40] After holding that the storyteller keeps faith in one's harmony with nature and its temporality, Benjamin returns to the image of the cathedral clock, writing:

> The storyteller keeps faith with it, and his eyes do not stray from that clockface and its revolving procession of creatures—a procession in which, depending on circumstances, Death is either the leader or the last wretched straggler.[41]

As opposed to the storyteller's "profane outlook," and secularized understanding of the inscrutable course of the world by way of natural history, there is, as we have already seen, the history-teller, or chronicler's eschatological interpretation of it on the basis of a plan of salvation.[42] As Benjamin argues in his analyses of Leskov's stories, the two narrative approaches cannot always be easily kept apart. In fact, he submits that "[i]n the storyteller the chronicler is preserved in changed form—secularized as it were."[43] Indeed, what is advanced about the place of death in relation to the procession of all natural creatures that revolve in front of the dial of the cathedral—an image that thus interlaces natural and eschatological time, profane and sacred history—acknowledges the fact that death is both the inexorable end of the living and that which, through the stories that it sanctions, allows for an afterlife. Through its stories, the afterlife in question is evidently a worldly one. Indeed, according to Benjamin all stories are embedded in the temporality of natural history in which death is not only the end of the life of finite creatures, but also the central event that crowns life by authoring stories through which the dying accomplishes a worldly afterlife, a worldly immortality, as it were, given that through these stories their life is remembered and retold as an unforgettable life.

Natural history, then, which the storyteller uses to interpret the course of the world, is the history of a nature in harmony with humanity, which, distinct from the status of nature in myth, makes of death an event that authorizes an afterlife—that is, a continuation of life within the profane web of social interconnectedness in the form of the stories told about it—rather than a mythic curse imposed on the living. Stories, sanctioned by a death appropriate to a creatural being—a public end of one's life—are what liberate the human beings from the spell of the mythical, and its order of fate.[44]

Before I turn to Hannah Arendt's politico-historical theory of stories, I must invoke my opening questions once again and extrapolate the, indeed, devastating consequences that follow from Benjamin's account of story and storytelling, particularly in the event that one is unable to tell one's story, or of authorizing another at the moment of death to do so. The question I raise based on the silence of so many survivors of the death camps regarding what they underwent is whether this silence, or rather muteness, is not the result of a definite impairment of what Benjamin calls a "seemingly inalienable possession" of the human being—namely, the faculty of telling the story of his or her life. What would be the implications and consequences of such an impairment from a Benjaminean perspective? At first glance, the historico-theological framework within which his theory of stories unfolds seems to provide a time and a place for the possibility that human beings would not be able to speak their situation aloud. Obviously, the time and place of such an inability is the archaic entanglement of the human being in the field of mythic forces. This time and place is, as we have seen, a state of pervasive muteness. Let us see, therefore, what it would mean for a muted human to relapse into such a state.

A being incapable of allowing its situation to speak would inexorably belong to a timelessly fallen nature. Such a being would be expelled from what Benjamin characterizes as "natural history" in which death becomes the crowning moment of the human being who, in that moment, becomes literally a story and is therein endowed with an ideal, hence, iterable form. By contrast, under the circumstances of fallen nature, a person is not only bereft of a voice but, strictly speaking, never even began a story that could be told or that, at the moment of death when the story becomes a whole, could have been bequeathed upon an other (such as a storyteller) to be retold by him or her. At the moment of death nothing unforgettable would have given this person's life the unity necessary to authorize its communication to others in the form of a story, and thus to secure the worldly afterlife of the person in all his or her singularity. In this case, the absence of natural time in the condition of the mythic entanglement in daemonic forces would have thwarted all possibility of forming a story as a complex misceneous—that is also, diaphanous formation to pass on, and to be retold. With the death, nothing of him or her would remain as transmissible, nothing unforgettable would be revealed in dying, and no authority would be transmitted to an other to pass on to posterity the memory of the dying. In other words, someone unable to pass on his or her story cannot be remembered and has thus never existed. His or her life would have ended before it began. It would have been a life that never took place.

The strictures of these archaic powers not only inhibit the ability of a life to be articulated in the form of a story—in a (ideal, and iterable) formation that survives its subject—they also entirely isolate the persons, who, by lacking a life story are unable to tell it and thus would be cast outside the intricate fabric that dialogically interconnects human beings who speak to one another by telling and listening to stories. Together with Lukacs, Benjamin characterizes the genre of the novel as reflective of the complete isolation of the modern human being. At one point, he evokes Arnold Bennett who speaks of such a human being without a story as a being who "had almost nothing in the way of real life."[45] But the novel is only symptomatic of the progressive loss of a hero's communicable experiences, and, hence, of story formation. However, the mute survivor of an extermination camp, severely impaired when it comes to storytelling, would have suffered an isolation incomparable to that of a character of a novel, who can still be shown to suffer from isolation and the loss of a world. By contrast, the one who has been violently subjected to the condition of being unable to transmit stories has absolutely no world, no horizon of a world, no horizon with respect to which the lack of a world could even be bemoaned. If world is constituted by the interrelations that are woven through acts of speaking and listening, of telling one's story and receiving counsel on how to continue that story by listening to the stories of others, an individual unable to tell his or her story would simply have no world whatsoever. The one who cannot tell his or her story cannot be spoken to and can speak to no one. For such an individual, no counsel is conceivable because this individual cannot let the situation speak and cannot, therefore, invite another to offer a story that might give advice. However, as we have seen, such counsel concerns the continuation of the story in which one finds oneself. But if one is deprived of a story, there is nothing to be continued. Having never begun a story, the 'life' of such a person would be deprived of all natural time—it would be at a standstill, stagnant. Counsel, Benjamin argues, helps to outwit the archaic forces of myth. Without a story that could invite counsel on how to carry on in the face of these overwhelming forces, the muted victim has no way to be freed from the strictures of myth.

But as we have seen, stories are the principal means by which the mute human being can be freed from this terrible state of ensnarement by the forces of myth. At this point let us recall Benjamin's distinction between two forms of muteness in the early essay "On Language as Such and on the Language of Man." In contrast to the humans who after the creation lived blissfully "in the pure spirit of language," nature is mute.[46] Yet, named by humans, this muteness itself "becomes bliss, only of lower degree."[47] Benjamin writes: "After the Fall, however, when God's word curses the ground, the appearance of nature is deeply changed. Now begins its other muteness, which is what we mean by the 'deep sadness of nature.'"[48] Overnamed in the hundred languages of humans, nature blocked from living in bliss as a result of being named, becomes overmuted, as it were. Indeed, overnaming is, Benjamin holds, "the deepest linguistic reason for all sadness and (from the point of view of the thing) for all muteness."[49] If it were endowed with language, fallen nature, Benjamin holds, would therefore lament the manifold of human languages, and the (secondary) muteness to which they reduce it. But nature is not only further muted by being overnamed, the sadness caused by this secondary muteness also "makes her mute."[50] The other muteness is thus a double muteness: one in which nature is further muted by the languages of humans, and one in which the sadness of nature deepens her own speechlessness. In Benjamin's words: "In all mourning there is the deepest inclination to speechlessness, which is infinitely more than the inability or disinclination to communicate."[51] And yet, as we have seen from "The Storyteller" even this doubly muted nature can as creatural nature be in complicity with humans in the struggle to pull free from the strictures of myth. The fairy tale and the story are testimony to this struggle. But another problem emerges with the muteness of both the soldiers of World War I, who returned mute from the front, and especially by the muteness of the survivors of the death camps. The muteness violently inflicted upon these groups amounts, indeed, to an impairment of the faculties of telling stories, which, because it is irrevocable, is thus incomparable to that of archaic muteness.[52] It is still another kind of muteness, a speechlessness that is the result not of a sadness, but caused by a debilitating senseless violence. Such irreversible reduction to a state of muteness would have to be one by forces far more archaic than those featured in Benjamin's historico-theological interpretation, forces that defy the distinction between the archaic past and the present, and hence the whole framework that Benjamin's theory presupposes.

The crucial importance of a third kind of muteness irreducible to either of the other two is highlighted by the fact that, as Benjamin makes it clear from the start, everything that storytelling accomplishes becomes evident only when it has already become a thing of the past. Only when it has basically ceased to exist, is it possible to muster the necessary distance and find the correct angle to define its function and accomplishments. The muteness of the soldiers of World War I returning from the trenches, is indicative of the rapid decline of storytelling and of the disappearance of the storyteller. Everything Benjamin establishes about stories and their tellers in the essay presupposes the new phenomenon of a muteness that does not allow for stories anymore. But implied as well in the decline in question is therefore also the withering of the possibility for human beings to be redeemed, whether in a theological or secular sense, through the form of the story. Furthermore, compared to the sadness of nature that can at least still "mourn" its speechlessness, mourning, in the context of this new muteness is also a possibility that has been taken away.

According to Benjamin's conception of story and storytelling, what makes it possible for human beings to free themselves from the strictures of myth is, on the one hand, their creatural status, and, on the other, the stories' verbal nature as a trace of the divine Word. As a result, only a being entirely bereft of all traces of its creatural status would be able to be muted to the point that freeing him- or herself from myth would no longer be an option. Such a person would already be dead, dead just like those inmates of the death camps who were called "Muselmänner"—that is, from a Benjaminean vista, robbed of the possibility as a creatural being of being redeemed through a story. Indeed, of the Muselmänner, who "form the backbone of the camp, an anonymous mass, continually renewed and always the same, of non-men who march and labor in silence," Levi remarks that "the divine spark [was] dead within them, already too empty to truly suffer."[53] Death in the camps consisted in the denial of death to the dying—that is, of death understood as the crowning moment of a life through which the dying person bequeaths the story of what has been the unforgettable nature of his or her life upon others. Only as such could death be pregnant with a promise of salvation, whether profane or religious. Without the possibility of having a story, such a person to whom death is denied would no longer be able to live on in the memory of those who survived. And, as Robert Antelme remarks, if in the camps "death has become the absolute evil," then it has also "ceased to be a possible opening towards God."[54]

3

SURVIVING FOR OTHERS
(Hannah Arendt)

EVEN THOUGH THE ISSUE OF STORIES IS BROACHED BY Hannah Arendt in several of her works, I limit myself here to her discussion of the topic in *The Human Condition*. However, since in her own translation of this work into German—*Vita activa oder Vom tätigen Leben*—she considerably reworked the original, I also, hereafter, have to regularly consider the latter version of this work. Arendt turns to the topic of the story in the opening sections 24 to 27 of the chapter devoted to action, which, significantly enough, features as an exergue the storyteller Isak Dinesen's statement on stories and telling stories, which reads: "All sorrows can be borne if you put them into a story or tell a story about them." The question of the story and storytelling thus emerges in Arendt's work through an intrinsic connection with the specifically human ability of action through deeds and words within the public domain—a faculty distinct from that of labor which the human shares with all animal life, and that of work, which although instrumental to creating a world, or the in-between, for plural men, can still be performed in isolation from the public world. In other words, in the realm of labor and, in contrast to what we encountered with Benjamin, in the realm of work, stories and storytelling have no place, or at least are not essentially tethered to these activities. By contrast, stories and storytelling pervade the domain of public life and action. It is here that they have their place and signification. Yet, even though all action is by definition public, and involves men in the plural, it is not political per se. Political action in the public domain concerns the objective interests of preserving and furthering this domain itself. But even though Arendt distinguishes between nonpolitical (without, however, specifying what it consists of) and political action, her explicit elaboration regarding action concerns primarily, if not exclusively, political life.[1] Hereafter it will thus be necessary to highlight the essential connection that links stories and storytelling to the eminently political activity in question.

However, anthropo-political considerations frame Arendt's developments of her theory concerning stories and storytelling. As is well known, her understanding of the political derives primarily from her critical assessment of political life in Greece for which she has frequently been accused of Graecophilia. Undoubtedly, her understanding of the political reaches back to the first emergence of it in the Greek polis. But life in the polis, rather than a standard or a measure, is just the foil against which she develops her conception of the political. Arendt's analysis in chapter 27 of *The Human Condition* of the way the Greeks solved the aporias of political action demonstrates that she does not in any way endorse their solution which consists, as will be seen, of bringing an order foreign to the political—the order of work—to bear on it, therein betraying the originality of what, indeed, had emerged for the first time in Greece. Paradoxically, the Greek solution to the aporias of action is a deceptive one, one which replaces stories with fabrications. Notwithstanding the fact that in *The Human Condition*, the Greek solution is explored after a detailed analysis of what is implied by action through words and deeds, it is, precisely, the shortcomings of Greek political life and of the Greeks' answer to the frailty of its institutions, that allow Arendt to develop the fundamentals of political life. Let me then try to sketch out as concisely as possible the rationale for creating a necessary link between action and the problematic of the story.

The material and worldly in-between, or open, in which human beings interact through action and speech to pursue objective interests that concern precisely this worldly in-between in which they move is created through work—that is, through the production of objects. Through their actions and speech regarding public matters in the worldly in-between, the agents in the public space also disclose to others *who* they are. In *Vita Activa*, in particular, Arendt evokes this "involuntary, or spontaneous, and additional revelation of the who of acting and speaking as an integral part of all, even the 'most objective' being-with-one-another."[2] This manifestation occurs in a second in-between, distinct from the first. In the American original she writes:

> Since this disclosure of the subject is an integral part of all, even the most "objective" intercourse, the physical, worldly in-between along with its interests is overlaid and as it were, overgrown [*durchwachsen und überwuchert*] with an altogether different in-between which consist of deeds and words and owes its origin exclusively to men's acting and speaking directly *to* one another. This second, subjective in-between is not tangible, since there are no tangible objects into which it could solidify; the process of acting and speaking can leave behind no such results and end products. But for all its intangibility, this in-between is no less real than the world of things we visibly have in common. We call this reality the "web" of human relationships, indicating by the metaphor its somewhat intangible quality.[3]

This second in-between, which grows from the first worldly one and overgrows it, is the arena in which the actors and speakers of the public realm reveal themselves as who they are, willingly or not, by appearing to others. Speaking together *about* things that concern the world they have in common, the agents engender, in Arendt's words, a "system of relations [*Bezugssystem*]," a fabric, or "web of relationships [*Bezugsgewebe*]"—a web, then, that is constitutive of the in-between of the actors themselves and through which they reveal themselves to others.[4] This web is the inevitable outcome of the involuntary self-disclosure of the agents in the public sphere through their words and deeds—in other words, of the relations that are woven between human beings over and above the pursuit of specific objective interests. This system of relations has a web-like quality—a quality that will be significant when it comes to the nature of stories, which originate, as we will see, precisely within this web.[5] However, before I can elucidate the specific role that stories play in this web of relationships, it is necessary to first address the status of the actors that interrelate in the worldly space in question.

By qualifying the agents in the public realm as actors—that is, as involved in an activity consisting of actions and speeches—several things are established from the start. For Arendt, action not only presupposes the plurality of men, but of men who are fundamentally equal and at the same time different from one another. Without being equal they could not understand each other, she remarks, and beyond this they must be equal insofar as they are all different from one another but must also remain equal without relinquishing their difference. Now, difference does not signify otherness (*Besonderheit*), Arendt claims. The category of otherness, or *alteritas*, as a universal characteristic of Being according to medieval philosophers, concerns only plurality in general. Hence it falls short of capturing not only the difference between living beings, but especially human difference. Arendt writes: "In man, otherness, which he shares with everything that is, and distinctness, which he shares with everything alive, becomes uniqueness [*Einzigartigkeit*], and human plurality is the paradoxical plurality of unique beings."[6] This distinctness of each human being based on his or her uniqueness—that is, being someone rather than a some-what—is not a function of him or her as a member of a living species, but as Arendt explains, of a second birth by which he or she arrives, or appears as a newcomer in the public world; in other words, as someone who stands for a new and unpredictable beginning. According to Arendt's theory of natality, the newcomer, who appears in the world, reveals a unique distinctness through precisely words and deeds. "Through them," she states, "men distinguish themselves instead of being merely distinct; they are the modes in which human beings appear to each other."[7] Action and speech are the prime, if not sole activities that qualify a being that appears as a new beginner in the midst of the public sphere of plural men, and through which such a being manifests his or her unique way of being human. From the start, this manifestation of the newcomer's uniqueness through action and speech—acts that are primordially and specifically human—shapes the relationship that he or she shares with equals. The reason for Arendt's distinction between nonpolitical and explicitly political action thus comes into view: Even before actions and speeches become political, they are, at first, activities through which the new beginner reveals himself. As Arendt observes,

> [i]n acting and speaking, men show who they are, reveal actively their unique personal identities and thus make their appearance in the human world, while their physical identities appear without any activity of their own in the unique shape of the body and the sound of the voice. This disclosure of "who" in contradistinction to "what" somebody is—his qualities, gifts, talents, and shortcomings, which he may display or hide—is implicit in everything somebody says and does.[8]

Needless to say, the uniqueness of the ones who reveal themselves to equal but also different plural others in the public space is accompanied by attempts to judge or to understand it. Determined by the question "Who are you?" it is a relationship intrinsic to action itself. But, therefore, the newcomer's actions must also from the outset be directed towards the plural world of different others. But such a thing is possible only if actions are accompanied by speech. Although agents also reveal themselves through their actions, Arendt insists that most acts must be accompanied by speech in order not to lose their subjects. There is, then, a greater affinity between speech and revelation than between action and revelation.[9] But Arendt's insistence that all action must be accompanied by speech in order for it to be relevant demonstrates the extent to which, already in advance of its political nature, the significance of action is tied to the open world of the many and relevant only if it is an intervention in that world. For action to be action in the sense that Arendt understands it, action must be identifiable by others as having been committed by a distinct *who* among them, which can be accomplished only by accompanying words.

Of the utmost importance in this context is the fact that the one who reveals him or herself through words and deeds to others in the public space does not do so intentionally and, above all, does not control the way he or she is perceived. The revelation in question is always involuntary, and cannot be avoided except by remaining completely silent and in perfect passivity. People cannot, Arendt argues, purposively disclose their identity

> as though one possessed and could dispose of this "who" in the same manner [one] has and can dispose of [one's] qualities. On the contrary, it is more than likely that the "who", which appears so clearly and unmistakably to others, remains hidden from the person himself, like the *daimon* in Greek religion which accompanies each man throughout

his life, always looking over his shoulder from behind and thus visible only to those he encounters.[10]

Indeed, in the Archaic Age, the kind of *daimon* that the Greeks believed to be "attached to a particular individual, usually from birth, [...] determin[ing], wholly or in part, his individual destiny," reflects the feeling that in certain situations at least, "a person or thing is not only itself but also something else."[11] Even though humans as beings capable of action are, in distinction from all other living things, "someones," rather than just representatives of the species "man," no one knows what constitutes his or her uniqueness, and cannot, therefore, purposively reveal it to others. Like one's individual *daimon*, the "who" one is manifests itself exclusively to others. The public space, or as Arendt writes in *Vita Activa*, "the world stage," is the space in which the unique "who" that one is takes objective shape for others through one's words and deeds.[12] Although action is *the* determining human activity in that, compared with labor and work, it alone ensures that someone can effectively be a unique being by beginning something new among others, he or she is this unique being exclusively for others. But acting and speaking "in sheer human togetherness," and therein revealing one's distinctness, also comes with a risk. It is impossible to calculate in advance how one will come across to others. Arendt writes: "Although nobody knows whom he reveals when he discloses himself in deed or word, he must be willing to risk the disclosure."[13] In the German version Arendt adds that only someone who is willing to continue to exist in such being-with-others who are distinct equals, and who is ready to take responsibility for the risk involved, can disclose to them who he or she is, and thus "renounce[e] the originary foreignness of the one who through birth has come into the world as a newcomer."[14] Only by foregoing through words and deeds one's "originary foreignness" in the public realm, exposing oneself to others, revealing one's daimon to them, does one enter the milieu of human interaction and become a distinct equal among equals.

By referencing the problematic of the daimon, I am already speaking of Arendt's theory of stories and storytelling. By evoking the daimon, Arendt points to a limit concerning self-disclosure that is constitutive of the very relationality between a newcomer and his or her equals in the public sphere, and which will prove to be the reason why such revelation inevitably takes shape in the form of stories woven by others. The stories to which the words and deeds give rise about the who in question, who remains hidden from him- or herself, will thus be stories of the agent's daimon. The implication is that stories about oneself are never stories told by oneself, but only by others. How indeed could one tell one's story if it is impossible to know oneself? As Arendt has already said, one does not dispose of one's who in the same way one disposes of one's qualities. But as we have also seen, all actions must be accompanied by speech through which the actor puts a name on the actions, and thus identifies him- or herself as someone whose story can possibly be conveyed by others. Without the actor's words there is nothing for others to remember about an action and to pass on. To the observation in *The Human Condition* that "[a]ction without a name, a 'who' attached to it, is meaningless," Arendt adds, in *Vita Activa*, that such action "becomes forgotten; there is nobody present whose story one could tell."[15] In other words, even though one's story will only be told by others, without speaking one does not leave one's "originary foreignness" behind, which in turn, would allow others to see one's daimon, and thus for them to be able to tell one's story—a story hidden from oneself. In anticipation of what we will see hereafter, I make the following observation: with this notion of the daimon, Arendt shows, of course, to what extent Greek thought and literature determines her understanding of the political, but as also becomes clear, this evocation of the daimon provides her with an opportunity to show to what degree the Greeks circumvented the implications of this very thought itself, and thus fail in her view the litmus test of the political.

Any agent in the public space makes his or her unique and irreplaceable who recognizable to others through words and deeds. Although this knowledge is the exclusive privilege of others, this does not mean that they are therefore capable of defining through language in an unequivocal manner *who* a someone is, for the simple reason that language only establishes *what* something is. In the German version of *The Human Condition*, Arendt even suggests that language's limitation, wherein it states merely *what* one is—thus responding only to the philosophical question *ti esti*—lessens one's exposition to one another. Stating what someone is, is above all, as she writes, a protective shield by language against "the bewildering unambiguity of Being-this-one-and-not-another."[16] The establishment of what someone is follows from a comparison with what that person has in common with others. But the question of who someone is aims at "the differentia specifica of being human, and this difference consists in the human being a someone whose Being-someone cannot be defined, because we cannot compare it with anything, and distinguish it qua Being-who from another kind of Being-who."[17]

The stakes of the impossibility of logically defining who someone is concern "the revelatory character without which action and speech would lose all human relevance."[18] Yet, although this impossibility is one of the reasons for the "the notorious uncertainty not only of all political matters, but of all affairs that go on between men directly, without the mediating, stabilizing, and objectifying medium of a world of things," this difficulty is also one that, as Arendt holds in *Vita Activa*, at the same time enriches the human intercourse and togetherness.[19] She does not specify what this richness consists of, but I believe she is thinking here of story formation and storytelling. In the domain of public and political life these formations and activities respond to the one aporia of human intercourse which "is perhaps the most fundamental" of all frustrations in that it concerns precisely the revelation of the person, without which acting and speaking lose their specific relevance.[20] Stories, indeed, are about the unique and distinct whos, who interact with one another in the public and political domain. Stories do what language—in its primary logical or cognitive use (that is, through predication)—cannot (and will not) accomplish—namely, articulate who an actor is through the way he or she spontaneously and involuntarily manifests him- or herself to others through words and deeds. Stories that formulate who someone is are a function of the agent's acts of speaking, talking, and wording (*Reden, Sprechen, Worte*), as opposed to language in the abstract (*Sprache*), which in its defining logical use can only name what somebody is. In a crucial move, Arendt thus distinguishes a function of language by which the who one is becomes muted—that is, inhibited from finding linguistic articulation (through which this who could be present to others) by being determined by categories that inextricably define him or her as a whatness—from another kind of language—namely, a prepredicative activity of language in the shape of activities such as speaking, talking, and wording, which are linguistic activities thoroughly within the domain of action. To what Aristotle calls the *logos apophantikos*, demonstrative speech—that is, the logos which constructs logically sound arguments— Arendt opposes another logos that is not structured by propositions capable of being true or false, a logos that Aristotle himself invokes in *De Interpretatione*, and which like prayer is not of the order of statement-making sentences. The study of this other logos belongs, as he points out, to the domain of poetry and rhetoric.[21] The other logos to which Arendt refers is, indeed, akin to the language Aristotle thematizes extensively in his analyses of citizens speaking with one another in the public realm, that is, in his Rhetoric.²² Within the sphere of action, this other form of language is the correlate of the speeches that accompany all action by an agent, more precisely, it is the language in which others articulate who the actor is. It is precisely from this practical dimension of speaking with one another that stories emerge.²³

At this juncture, let us remind ourselves of the complex web of relationships characteristic of human affairs within which the stories concerning its agents are enacted, or rather, presented (*dargestellten*), as the title of chapter 25 of *Vita Activa* holds. Given language's failure in its logical use to define a who, a consideration of this relationship between the web of relations and the stories that are presented within it might put us on the way to an understanding of how language, in its narrative use, is able to form an agent's who. In stories, language, rather than defining what somebody is, reveals or articulates who someone is for others, and it does so precisely through its narrative function. Language here forms stories regarding an agent's who as it is perceived by others. As opposed to the agent's speech that accompanies his or her actions, story formation and storytelling are the language of the other, as it were. In telling, language, then, is no longer a logical but becomes an eminently practical activity. Unlike logical language it is not distinct from that about which it makes its propositions; language in the form of storytelling is an intrinsic part of the web of relations in the public realm. In order to explore this practical dimension of language, I turn to the following lines where Arendt submits that

> [t]he realm of human affairs, strictly speaking, consists of the web of human relationships which exists wherever men live together. The disclosure of the "who" through speech, and the setting of a new beginning through action, always fall into an already existing web where their immediate consequences can be felt. Together they start

a new process which eventually emerges as the unique life story of the newcomer, affecting uniquely the life stories of all those with whom he comes into contact.[24]

This statement makes clear that the self-disclosing speech of the agent is part and parcel of the web of relations within which it occurs. Indeed, in proposing something new, the newcomer's initiatives are not only addressed to others from the start, the newcomer also calls on others to help him or her carry out the initiative, and thus these initiatives doubly affect the life and life-stories of others. In *Vita Activa* Arendt follows up on this passage with a decisive comparison. Since the web of human relations always precedes both the actions through which a newcomer makes a new beginning and the speeches through which he or she reveals him- or herself as a new beginner, the new beginning that's made and the unique who that's revealed,

> are like threads that are being driven into an already woven pattern [*wie Fäden sind, die in ein bereits vorgewebtes Muster geschlagen werden*], and which in a unique way transform in turn the web by affecting all the life-threads with which they come into contact within this web. Once the threads are spun to their end, they give rise to clearly recognizable patterns, that is, they can be narrated as life-stories.[25]

The actions, but also the speech of the actor through which the actor reveals him or herself, are threads spun within a web of human interactions.[26] They are never acts that impact the web in question from the outside—hence never acts made in isolation—but that always originate from within the weave—and are "in constant contact" with it.[27] In the same way as the actions, the involuntary self-disclosures that ultimately crystallize as life stories, capable of being told and retold, have an unmistakably practical (as opposed to logical and theoretical) nature. However, before putting this dimension of stories into further relief, I wish to draw attention to the close relationship between the web-like structure of human interaction and the stories, which in turn, are like webs woven by others from the threads driven by an agent's speeches into the preexisting web. One weave is part and parcel of another one; stories arise out from and into the web woven through human relations, which they thus transform. It is from such stories that what has been called a "second in-between" of the world is made up.[28] And just like the second in-between, which has been qualified as intangible despite its reality, the stories that belong to it are equally intangible and yet very real.

As Arendt reminds us, "every individual life between birth and death can eventually be told as a story with beginning and end."[29] Like for Schapp and for Benjamin, every human being must have a life story to have been a human being. But similar to Benjamin's account of the formation of stories, this story, for Arendt, is not simply the product of the individual it concerns. In Arendt's account stories are not something made by the individual at all and in fact possess a level of ideality—as their characterization as intangible indicates—that does not originate in the individual's intentions and consciousness. The stories concerning actors in the public realm have an ideality that is bestowed upon the life of individuals solely by others. Precisely because the actions and self-revelation of the new beginner intervene in "an already existing web of human relations, with its innumerable, conflicting wills and intentions," the actor almost never achieves in purity, as Arendt observes, what was initially intended.[30] Negatively speaking, stories come into being because the presence of others makes it impossible to realize, fully and purely, the intentions and projections of consciousness. They are not products of the individual's consciousness. An individual has a story only because he or she is not alone. In *Vita Activa* she adds that only because acting consists in driving one's thread into a fabric that one has not made oneself, can it bring forth stories with the same naturalness (*Selbstverständlichkeit*) with which work produces things and objects. The most originary product of action is not the realization of goals and purposes preconceived in advance, but the story that it did not intend at the beginning, and that comes into being when determined goals are pursued. The stories may present themselves to the actor himself at first as only secondary by-products of his doings. What in the end finally remains in the world, are not the impulses that motivated him, but the stories of which he was the cause.[31]

If in the end it is these stories rather than the actor's intentions that survive, it is also because as formations that are not of the order of an individual consciousness, they have an enduring ideality of their own. But their lasting reality must not be confused with their material forms in the shape, for example, of documents, monuments, or archives. The distinction Arendt makes here between stories in their living reality and stories as material sediments of social interactions, although not always made in the desired explicitness, is of critical importance to her understanding of the topic. Ultimately, stories are not what they are insofar as they are reified stories—in other words, things like other things—but only insofar as they have a living reality due to their being constituted and told within the social web. Arendt writes:

> They themselves, in their living reality, are of an altogether different nature than these reifications [the reference is to the objective forms they can take]. They tell us more about their subjects, the "hero" in the center of each story, than any product of human hands ever tells us about the master who produced it, and yet they are not products

properly speaking. Although everybody started his life by inserting himself into the human world through action and speech, nobody is the author or producer of his own life story. In other words, the stories, the results of action and speech, reveal an agent, but this agent is not an author or producer. Somebody began it and is its subject in the twofold sense of the word, namely its actor and sufferer, but nobody is its author.[32]

Stories in their "living reality" are not produced, made, or fabricated as are their reified forms.[33] They are not the outcome of acts of *poiesis*, neither by the agent, since the sole subject of the story is what he or she involuntarily reveals, nor by the others who experience or encounter the agent only as the agent discloses him- or herself to them. Undoubtedly, a story begins with a newcomer's initiative, and what the newcomer involuntarily makes known through the individual acts. Others, as well, are congenitally involved in its formation, but this involvement is not in any way a modality of making. The stories that originate with the experiences of the agent are lived stories. They consist, on the one hand, of a lived web woven by what an agent involuntarily reveals about himself through the acts by which he inserts himself into the plural human world—stories that the agent, rather than controlling, "lives," at best as something that happens to the agent without his or her knowledge, and at worst, that he or she suffers. On the other hand, stories consist of the acts through which others within the human world experience, and thus also shape, what the agent brings of the self into public view while pursuing interests concerning the common world. The subject of a story is thus not the private but the public person, the person as he or she acts and speaks with others. Rather than through poiesis, stories in their living reality thus come into being through the weaving together of different strands of acts of *praxis* within the web of relations that make up the second worldly in-between.[34] They are the inevitable byproducts of human *praxis*, products that in their "living reality" have a status different from that of works. A life story, then, is never something made by a sovereign subject. It cannot even be directly imputed to someone since *who* this someone is will become tangible only ex post factum through action and speech—that is, through the story to which he or she will have given rise. Arendt writes: "*Who* somebody is or was we can know only by knowing the story of which he is himself the hero."[35] If, then, "every individual life between birth and death can eventually be told as a story with beginning and end," it is also clear that although the beginning of a story is that of an individual's appearance in the public world, and its end that of his or her disappearance, both beginning and end are not within the power of the individual, but categories of the second in-between.[36]

Before returning to the problematic of the daimon—that is, to one's true self at the core of the stories engendered by others—two aspects of action still need to be addressed, which, according to Arendt, bear on the story that rises from involuntary self-revelation and its experience by others. The first concerns the inescapably boundless consequences of an action that result from the fact that its initiator acts within a plurality of men themselves capable of action and, hence, of reaction. Thanks to this boundlessness of the consequences of action, the actor "is never merely a 'doer' but always and at the same time a sufferer. To do and to suffer are like opposite sides of the same coin, and the story that an act starts is composed of its consequent deeds and sufferings."[37] I will not broach here in as detailed a fashion as it merits Arendt's discussion, drawing on Greek history and philosophical thought, of how strongmen, rulers, and sovereigns monopolize action in an attempt to ward off unwanted consequences of action with the effect of perverting its very nature. Nor will I linger on her discussion of the inevitability of the limitations that a state and its institutions impose from the outside on the boundlessness of action if the possibility of action is to be maintained. By contrast, I wish to focus in a somewhat more extensive way on the second outstanding aspect of action, closely related to the first—namely "its inherent unpredictability."[38] "The fact that no one is ever capable of fully assessing, or predicting [*übersehen*, i.e., oversee, or estimate] the consequences of his own deed," is, as Arendt states in *Vita Activa*, intimately linked to the story that begins with each action.[39] In *The Human Condition* she writes:

> This is not simply a question of inability to foretell all the logical consequences of a particular act, in which case an electronic computer would be able to foretell the future, but arises directly out of the story which, as the result of action, begins and establishes itself as soon as the fleeting moment of the deed is past.[40]

The unpredictability of the consequences of a deed has to do neither with the contingent limitations of an actor, nor with the finitude as a human being, which prevent him or her from foreseeing them. Rather, the unpredictability in question is a function of the story itself, a story that inevitably comes into being at the moment an action is over. Indeed, this story outlasts the deed, gains a life of its own, and is no longer under the control of the doer of the deed because it is in the nature of a story to be spun by others and to be spun further by others. As we have already seen, a story is never authored by the doer of the deed that triggers it. Here, however, Arendt makes the additional point that the nature of stories is such that the full meaning of the deed of which they tell cannot be predicted by its doer. In a sizeable addition in the German version of *The Human Condition*, which seems to suggest that, even though there is no acknowledgment, Arendt may in the meantime have become familiar with Schapp's work, she explains:

> The unpredictability of the consequences [of an action] belongs to the course of the story that inevitably has been produced as a result of an action. The unpredictability constitutes the suspense (*Spannung*) proper to this story, that stretches (*spannt*) over a whole human life, and keeps it going, without which this life would literally collapse from boredom. This suspense in which we await the denouement (*Ausgang*) of a story, contributes to our unswerving adjustment to and orientation toward the future, even though we know all too well that the only certain end of what is to come is one's own death. The fact that as living beings we are at all capable of existing with death in front of us, and that we do not comport ourselves in such a way as if we waited only for the final execution of the death sentence that was pronounced at the moment we were born, may be linked to the fact that we are always singularly entangled (*verstrickt*) in a story that keeps us in suspense, and whose end we do not know.[41]

The supplemental point made in this passage regarding life stories that result from the human being's arrival in the world and the beginning of something new, and which are woven by all those who, with the newcomer, are in this world, is that such a story is completed only with the newcomer's departure from the public world. This departure is of the order of a disappearance. Indeed, in the same way as the appearance of the newcomer in public life is not a biological event, the newcomer's eventual disappearance from it is not caused by death as a physiological end. But that eventual disappearance marks all the events of a life as moments in a story that not only keeps us in suspense, but whose suspense is owed to the fact that we are stretched (*ge-spannt*)—Heidegger would have said *erstreckt*—between a beginning and a sure end. The suspense characteristic of stories is actually of life itself, but of life in a narrated form. Arendt's reference to one's being entangled in stories highlights, precisely, the human being's directional stretching toward an end that he or she does not know and will never have known. She writes:

> The reason why the suspense of life, the élan as it were of the beginning given with birth, can endure until death, is due to the fact that the signification of every story reveals itself fully only at the moment the story has come to an end, in other words, that during our lifetime we are entangled in a story whose outcome we don't know.[42]

Even though suspense is a narrative category, it is also in a certain sense the specifically human way of living one's finitude, of experiencing every event in one's life as marked by the inevitable disappearance of oneself from the world. But inevitably only others will witness the end of a life story, since the story of the living is never yet a story because it is still in suspense. Only for others are there life stories because stories are stories only on the condition of having an end.[43] However, these incomplete stories of the living are not stories at all. Only the individual's disappearance from the web of relations gives his or her life the form and the totality without which a story is not a story. In her concluding reflections on the constitutive end of stories, Arendt makes the following observation at the end of chapter 26 of *The Human Condition*: "Even though stories are the inevitable results of action, it is not the actor but the storyteller who perceives and 'makes' the story."[44] In *Vita Activa* these ending lines are reworded as follows: "Even though stories that can be told are the sole univocally manifest results of human action, it is not the acting agent who recognizes and tells the story that he has caused as a story, but the storyteller who is entirely uninvolved in it."[45]

While exploring the link between the unpredictability of the outcome of an action and the undesigned revelatory character of action and speech, in which one discloses one's self without ever either knowing oneself or being able to calculate beforehand *whom* one reveals, and which generates the story about the agent whose full meaning becomes manifest only when it has ended, Arendt evokes "[t]he ancient saying that nobody can be called *eudaimon* before he is dead."[46] After having restored the original meaning of this term, which admittedly is hard to translate and to explain, she avers that rather than to happiness or beatitude, it refers to "something like the well-being of the *daimon* who accompanies each man throughout life, who is his distinct identity, but appears and is visible only to others."[47] According to Archaic Greek beliefs, the daimon is, from the beginning, the one who one is. According to Aristotle to be *eudaimon* and to have been *eudaimon* also refers to "a lasting state of being which is neither subject to change nor capable of effecting change."[48] But in Arendt's interpretation of the daimon and his or her *eudaimonia*, the daimon is the one who, in the end, one will fully have been, and who at that moment can enjoy well-being because the totality of one's actions and speeches will finally have made the who one is into a complete and identical self visible to others, who, at the same time, can then also assess the meaning of one's story. Who one is, is not fully graspable or tangible either to oneself or to others until one has departed from life. At that moment, the living one who one has been will become tangible in the shape of a story, capable of being told and retold. While "disclosing itself intangibly in act and speech," one's who becomes tangible—that is, "a palpable entity"—in the German version Arendt says, "potentially like a thing among other things"—only after a life story has come to its end.[49] Caution is necessary in evaluating what Arendt means to say. The fact that who one is and has been becomes tangible only at the end of one's life story does not mean that it has already become a thing among things, but only potentially so. A life story becomes a thing among other things when it is reified in the form of a document or monument, or when it is no longer anything more than just a story.⁵⁰ At that moment life stories are just departed lives, things like other things, and hence part of the arsenal of things produced through work that fill the in-between of the world in which humans act. But before this inevitably happens, the story is a living story to its end, and is lived as such by those who, in the second in-between, survive an individual's disappearance from the web of relations.

At this point the main features of Arendt's conception of stories, and the specific conditions under which they arise, are fully in place. As I pointed out, Arendt's account of the nature of stories is framed by anthropo-political considerations. I suggested that even though Arendt reaches back to the origins of the political in Greece, the positive outlines of her conception of action as the most political activity and the formation of stories as its correlate derive from a critique, rather than a wholesale endorsement, of what she terms "the Greek solution of, or the Greek way out of, the aporias of action."⁵¹ As we have already seen, it is not possible for an actor in the public and political domain to "consciously aim[s] at being 'essential.'"⁵² In Arendt's words:

> [W]hat for an individual might be the ultimate commitment beyond which there can be no further commitment, appears in the weave of relations between human beings as only a new weft or woof [*Einschlag*], which, at best, only outlines a beginning, or a new model which can change its physiognomy in still uncountable ways before it is finished because it intersects with the innumerable threads of those who continue to weave it to its end.⁵³

Yet, by aiming precisely at being "essential," and at effectively leaving behind a story that they controlled, the Greek heroic figures—that is, the Greek role models incarnating *arete*, or virtue—sought to outwit the unpredictability of the consequences of public and political interaction. Achilles is a case in point. It was his figure, Arendt contends elsewhere, who "in his increasing effort to excel, always to be the best and so gain immortal glory, that remained the standard that distinguished the Greek in his polis as a human type."[54] Indeed, Achilles, according to Homer's *Iliad*, decides to kill Hector, who had slain his friend Patroclus, in full knowledge that he himself would meet an early death of which he had been warned by his horse, and the dying Hector as well. Indeed, by expressly choosing to perform a supreme act of this kind, which he could not survive, hence, "a short life and premature death," Achilles successfully eludes the possible consequences of his deed, thus leaving behind a story and an identity of which he remained "the indisputable master."[55] Arendt muses:

> What gives the story of Achilles its paradigmatic significance is that it shows in a nutshell that *eudaimonia* can be bought only at the price of life and that one can make sure of it only by foregoing the continuity of living in which we disclose ourselves piecemeal, by summing up all of one's life in a single deed, so that the story of the act comes to its end together with life itself.[56]

Now apart from noting, with Arendt, the "highly individualistic" way in which the Greek sought to control their singular identity, as a result of which the actors sought to circumvent the consequences of acting within the web of public and political interrelations, the question I wish to ask is whether the stories that they bequeathed to those who survived them share any of the qualities of living stories, or whether they are not from the very start already artifacts among other things.

Although Arendt acknowledges that notwithstanding his successful attempt to block further changes to his story, Achilles "remains dependent on the storyteller, poet, or historian, without whom everything he did remains futile." She remarks that he is the only "hero," and therefore the hero par excellence, who delivers into the narrator's hand the full significance of his deed, so that it is as though he had not merely enacted the story of his life but at the same time also "made" it.[57]

Unlike Benjamin's storyteller, Arendt's storyteller is not a craftsman (who leaves an imprint on the stories about foreign places and the past that he or she weaves for his or her immediate contemporaries), but more like someone who records life stories for posterity. To this storyteller Achilles hands over his completed story. Achilles, the hero par excellence, is the artisan of his own stories in which the storyteller cannot change or add anything. By aiming from the start to disclose himself through a deed which he could not survive, and thus to prevent others from changing its meaning, he was able to craft his own story, and thus control what would be remembered as his daimon. For this reason, Arendt holds in the German version of *The Human Condition* that the Greek hero is not only the doer of his deed, but at the same time "the author of the story that results from it," or in the original version, that Achilles himself "makes"—that is, produces or fabricates like a craftsman his own story.[58] In short, the Greek solution to the aporias of action, paradigmatically illustrated by Achilles, would thus consist in applying a model originating in the sphere of work to the formation of one's identity, a process, which on the basis of action should have been left to be performed by the multitudinous others. In the German version of *The Human Condition* Arendt concludes that "[i]t is as if Achilles had dared to peer over his own shoulder in order to see his *daimon*, and what he saw was personified courage."[59] Yet, and Arendt is seemingly unaware of this, by revealing himself as "personified courage," Achilles hands over to posterity only a *quality* that he possesses, rather than his who, of which stories are made. By replacing his essence as a who with a quality such as courage, Achilles's answer to the aporias of public action becomes an intrinsic part of the deceptive Greek solution. To sum up, what Arendt's statement suggests is that Achilles did not only take the story of his own identity into his own hands, just like an artisan who produces a clay pot in full isolation from the public space of human interaction, thus offsetting the unpredictability characteristic of the realm of action, but also committed an act of hubris with the explicit intention to exchange his life for the immortality that only the gods enjoy.[60]

In short then, if Achilles indeed "became the prototype of action for Greek antiquity, and, influenced, in the form of the so-called agonal spirit, the passionate drive to show one's self in measuring up against others that underlies the concept of politics prevalent in the city-states," it becomes evident that, for Arendt, the Greek solution for the aporias of action was a way to escape from the boundlessness and, in particular, the unpredictability of the realm in question, an attempt to destroy "the very substance of human relationships," which the Greeks had been the first to recognize.[61] By bringing to bear a model foreign to the domain of action on the formation of stories, the stories fabricated by the heroes were not living stories in a strict sense. Self-disclosure is not the reason of action in a proper sense but, as seen, only its by-product. However, by making self-disclosure through actions, and hence one's stories in the Greek political sphere, an overriding factor, action is also no longer strictly speaking action, and stories no longer stories. The Greek solution to the aporias of action within the fabric of human relations is thus, in truth, and paradoxically, a highly un-Greek solution.

As we have seen, for Arendt, stories are made by others. One does not make them intentionally oneself, except by looking over one's shoulder and thus handing them down prefabricated to the storyteller. But what also transpires from this account is that the one who, like Achilles, fabricates his or her story by neutralizing all the possible changes that this story would undergo if it were followed up by other actions, has made him- or herself into a storyteller who in death passes the story on to the storyteller, poet, or historian to be remembered. In other words, telling one's own story is possible only if this story is no longer, strictly speaking, a story, but a product of ambiguous making.

For Arendt, genuine stories are the by-product of action within a public and political domain, and, furthermore, the product of others. In returning, then, to our opening problematic—the inability of many survivors of the death camps to relate their stories—it is first important to recall that even though subjects are from the start entangled in stories, it is not the subjects themselves who tell them. No one can tell one's own life story because it only comes to completion with the death of its protagonist. Therefore, the issue of being incapable of telling does not arise in the context of Arendt's account of stories and storytelling. If, however, as is the case with Achilles, it is the subject of the story who passes it on by telling it to the storyteller, these stories are no longer stories in a genuine sense. Individuals are entangled in stories only insofar as they belong as unique human beings to the public and political realm within the web of which their actions and speeches render the formation of stories visible or readable only by others. But the detainees in the camps were from the start deprived of a public space of togetherness, and by the same token of the action and speech constitutive of it. No public communal space existed in the camps, not only between the SS and the detainees, which is obvious, but not between the detainees themselves either. In other words, from the very outset they were robbed of their unique singularity, which, as the condition for acting and speaking, is also the condition for involuntarily exposing themselves to stories woven by others. If as survivors of the camps they could be said to have been unable to tell their stories, it is thus, first, because they were inhibited from having one for their equals, which could have then been told about them. Prevented from acting and speaking due to the absence of a public space, the detainees had no possible way of revealing their public identity to others. No daimon accompanied them anymore. No daimon was to be seen by others. To evaluate the implications of being dispossessed of a daimon, it is important to recognize that for Arendt, as for Benjamin, stories are, first and foremost, lingual formations that bestow upon a given human life a certain ideality—a tangible ideality that is, an "ideality" thoroughly immanent to the human web of relations—that makes what is unique, irreplaceable, and unrepeatable, repeatable—that is, a living story—before it becomes nothing but a story. It is this very understanding of the nature of the story—an understanding that characterizes Arendt's theory in much greater depth than those of Schapp or Benjamin—which must guide us in judging what, accordingly, the implications are of being denied a story.

Using Arendt's understanding of living versus reified stories, we can see that the detainees who were deprived of the words and deeds necessary to disclose themselves to others were precluded from a form of life that, because of its tangible ideality, would have been repeatable, transmissible, or communicable. Life in stories is an intrinsic element of what Arendt qualifies as the second in-between characteristic of the world, and thus constitutes the uniquely human life. Undoubtedly, every life is thoroughly unique, but this uniqueness is smothered from the beginning unless it has a story. To have a story amounts to having been allowed the minimal ideality necessary in order to partake in what transcends the species man—namely, human community, and in particular, its political constitution. Yet this is precisely what was taken from the detainees upon entering the camps. Being denied the possibility of having their story formed by others, they were thus rejected from the human condition of being-together-with-others.

A different, but not unrelated strain in Arendt's theory of stories remains to be discussed: namely, the importance of death for the completion of a story. Death by extermination does not retrospectively provide a victim with an identity because death by extermination does not allow the essence of the who that one will have been to find a form of completeness. To begin with, death by extermination is not a *disappearance* from the public realm. On the contrary, such death rescinds the victim's appearance in the world in the first place, and consequently also the possibility of disappearance. Death by extermination of the inmates of the camps conformed with their systematic dehumanization by denying them the defining feature of being human—namely that of having appeared to others in the world—and thus of having begun to spin a story that would have lifted them to the status of having been unique, irreplaceable human beings.[62] In other words, such death consists in putting an end not only to what Arendt in her earlier work still calls "spontaneity" or freedom, which is "linked to life as such in the sense of simply remaining alive," but also to what she later calls "natality," which designates the human being's entrance into the entirely un-natural sphere of human interaction—an entrance, which, in distinction from a birth into the biological family, is, as Arendt's talk of a "second birth" indicates, spontaneous, in short, self-initiated by the human being's "appearance" in the world.[63]

But what of those who escaped extermination but who nonetheless were unwilling or unable to speak about what they had suffered? Within the frame of Arendt's elaborations on the nature of stories, what could be the meaning of their silence or muteness? What, in this context, are the implications of being unable tell? As we have seen, for Arendt, all action and speech within public space comes with the inevitable risk of not coming across to others in the way one intended. Could this mean that the survivors of the camps have just been unwilling to take this risk, or that their ability to take the risk of being misunderstood or misjudged, has been fundamentally crippled? For Arendt, to take this risk is an intrinsic condition of public, and hence of truly human life. It follows that the muteness of the survivors, who in the camps were refused the dignity of uniqueness and, hence, a story, apart from resisting clichés of what they had undergone—stories, in short, that in no possible way could approximate their experience—might be a response to the risk of being denied a story once again. By not speaking of the terrible ordeals of the camps, the former detainees may be attempting to resist the appropriation of their "stories" by others. In other words, their muteness, perhaps, resists the dis-appropriation of their self-disclosure, by which the survivors' speech would be turned by others into stories in which the survivors would not recognize themselves.

But following Arendt's understanding of the nature of stories, according to which stories are not of one's own making but are made by others, the survivor could not have had a story to begin with. Muteness, thus, is also one more way to resist having had something—a story—that only others could possibly have produced. It is an ultimate refusal of the ultimate affront of being deprived, again, of what one was denied in the camps. Could one, then, not wager to say that the survivor's silence might originate in an inveterate knowledge gained about how to remain mute after having been denied a voice?

If one follows Arendt's exploration of the nature of the story to its fullest conclusions, the survivor's muteness regarding the horrors he or she has undergone is not simply an inability. Nor is it an attempt to keep something inexpressible a secret. The refusal to have a story for others might, in fact, be the paradoxical testimony to an irreducible remainder of singular uniqueness. Within the public space of speaking with one another it would be the minimal demonstration and manifestation of what makes the human being human. In an age flooded by stories—indicative of the fact that stories in Arendt's sense have become fewer and fewer—the survivor's refusal to have a story, this muteness, is a muteness that demands not to be questioned. Withdrawing from the request to provide meaning and transparency by way of a story to what has been incomprehensible from the start, to the victim especially, the victim's muteness is the only possible answer. As such it calls for unconditional respect.

POSTLIMINARIES
Storytelling and World Loss

THAT SOME OF THOSE WHO RETURNED FROM THE CAMPS successfully cast what they underwent into a story about what they suffered in no way challenges the fact that many of the survivors were incapable of telling the story of their ordeal. But even those who told stories did not tell the untellable. This is also the case of those who, like Elie Wiesel, wrote against the silence of the victims. Though seemingly capable of facing their memories, their stories remain documents of muteness. To use a Derridean expression, one can perhaps characterize their written memoirs as forms of "mute writing."[1] The muteness that pervades the accounts of those who have been capable of speech demands respect as well. In narratives about the holocaust, the muteness in question is particularly obvious in those accounts where the form of the story has been transformed. The pauses, breaks, black spaces, lacunae in some of the narratives, such as Kertesz's, or the broken syntax in the poetry of Paul Celan, for example, are the sites in which the muteness of the victims finds a, however tenuous, inscription.

As our analysis of storytelling has demonstrated no dominant mode or figure of representation, nor any identical and determinable displacement or interruption of such modes or figures is up to the task of the representation of the senseless violence endured by the survivors of the camps. Throughout the essay this question of the possibility of the representation of senselessness has been a constant issue. But by now it should be evident that in the precise context of an exploration of the form of the story in relation to the senselessness of the holocaust no unambiguous response is possible, and not even desirable. The muteness of many of the survivors is their singular way of representing what happened to them. The written accounts of some of them are the equally singular way—ways that alter the traditional form of narrative—of representing the senselesnesss and incomprehensibility of what they underwent. Undoubtedly a formal analysis of how they have individually addressed the possibility of representing how they lived the disaster would be warranted. But from such analyses no overall conception for representation of their experience can be given and should not be sought. Any canon of rules for the representation of what they lived through is more than problematical since it levels the unique way in which each survivor accomplishes his or her "mute writing." Any such general conception would end in the effacement of the aporia that each singular writer had to address, and addresses in his or her own unique way.

In any event, in order to write or tell the muteness that testifies to what has been done to human beings in the camps, and which is the most terrifying way in which they can continue to testify to their integrity as human beings, the form of the story presupposed by all three theories on stories and storytelling discussed here demands a radical recasting. Interruptions, displacement, transformations are certainly ways in which this is achieved. By the same token, philosophy's traditional evaluation of the difference between its discourse and that of stories of such kind also requires revisiting.

✦ ✦ ✦

The stories that the survivors of the camps have been unable to tell—stories that have condemned them to having no stories because they are at the origin of their muteness—are not stories among others. However, they are not, therefore, unique, or singular stories. Indeed, as stories that have resulted in their subject's muteness, they have deprived him or her of a respective singularity and, as such, they cannot themselves be singular stories. They are stories of an exceptional nature because the senselessness of which they would speak depleted them of a possible narrative form. They are exceptional not only because of their lack of singularity, but also in that they lack what characterizes stories in essence—namely, to be communicated, to be told. These stories, because they are not stories, lack the tendency toward a listener. Therefore, although it is apparent that none of the three theories we have considered has a place for them, the very possibility of these non-stories may challenge these theories by questioning from within the assumptions these theories make about stories and about their telling.

✦ ✦ ✦

Does the assumption that a life is not human when it cannot be narrated not become problematic when just one story, which cannot be exchanged, coexists with other less exceptional, hence, tellable stories? Undoubtedly, before their incarceration, inmates lived their stories and were entangled in the stories of others. What, indeed, is the relation between these stories, prior to the one of the extermination camps and the untellable story of the latter? Does the one untellable story leave the tellable ones intact? Or, on the contrary, would a story so senseless and horrendous as to prevent it from having the form of a story not inevitably affect a person's previous stories, their quality as stories, and thus infringe on this individual's possession of world? If, indeed, the untellable story with which the survivors have lived has the effect that with it every story has, in Kertesz's words, "come to an end, that all our stories are untellable stories," then this is an inevitable question.² Let us remind ourselves that a story is a tangible way through which one can encounter and be encountered by others. The world of the survivor, whose faculty to make sense of experiences has been inhibited, would be an abstract world in which only abstract entities hold power, entities which no longer hold any relation to other entities. Would such abstraction not cast a long shadow over the entirety of what can be told?

✦ ✦ ✦

The three theories on storytelling in light of which I have confronted the holocaust survivors' inability to communicate their experiences—those of Wilhelm Schapp, Walter Benjamin, and Hannah Arendt—are theories developed independently of the context that interests us here. Yet if these three theories have helped to raise the question of how the inability to form stories can or cannot be accounted for by them, it is all the more important to sharply demarcate the specific frameworks within which they approach their subject. These frameworks or horizons within which these theoretical accounts expand on stories and storytelling not only color, in depth, their specific understanding of the topic, but also shape in distinct ways what, from their angle, the consequences would be of having one's ability of storytelling aborted.

In the case of Schapp, entanglement in stories is the primary mode through which a human being has a world, and the way in which, in this world, the human being is co-entangled in the stories (and worlds) of others. Unable to tell his or her story, the holocaust survivor lacking a story also lacks a world and is thus also prevented from encountering others through their stories. In the case of Benjamin's *The Storyteller*, having been muted to the point of having no story means to have been radically stripped of one's creatural nature. Without a story, it would not only not be possible to elude the archaic powers of guilt, but a person in such a condition would have been depleted forever of the possibility of redemption, whether understood in profane or religious terms. Having been muted, unable to accompany one's actions with words through which others can weave a living story about oneself, one would, according to Arendt, not only have been denied participation in the public world, but also of the fundamental existential condition of being-with-others. More fundamentally even, deprived of the specifically human activity of acting, or initiating new beginnings, one would ultimately have been deprived of the very possibility of appearing. In sum then, having nothing to tell and lacking anything that could be told about him or her, the muted survivor would have been condemned to be *without a world*. Having been denuded of a creatureliness, the survivor, unable to tell a story, would have been forced to *forego the promise of a redemption*, and finally, the lack of a living story would have *stripped him or her from appearing in the first place.*

Undoubtedly, having been robbed of a world, of being capable of appearing within the world to others, and, furthermore, being depleted by the muteness to which one has been reduced of the possibility of a redemption that all of nature—but especially the human being insofar as he or she occupies the highest rung within its order—can hope for, the human being would have been stripped from what these theories on stories and storytelling consider the essence of the human being. As the title of Levi's book *If This Is a Man* (*Se questo e un uomo*) indicates, the dehumanization by human beings of other human beings in the camps consisted in depleting the victim of everything that could remind him or her of belonging to the human species, whether biologically or theologically. The absence of a mark of interrogation in the title confirms the finding. The muteness of the victim, the lack of a story, except the story of not having had one for the self or for others, is the ultimate index of the indeterminateness to which the victim—neither something living nor something dead—had been reduced.

These are where the conclusions of the three different theories, pressed to account for the muteness of the holocaust survivors, inexorably converge. They are conclusions necessarily ushered in by all three theories because of their theologico-metaphysical and humanist underpinnings. But do these underpinnings not at the same time shelter these theories from acknowledging the possibility that what has happened in the camps, that which resists all telling, could put the theories of stories and their humanist implications radically into question? Is it not surprising, at least, that the possibility of a complete breakdown of the formation of stories and storytelling is not even something to be considered by Schapp; or that when, in Benjamin, the assumption that story formation and telling are inalienable possessions of the human being becomes questionable, storytelling nonetheless remains the horizon within which the dispossession in question is theorized? Perhaps only in Arendt might one find—but in different contexts—an acknowledgment that the muteness of the survivors calls for another approach, since the abyssal horror of the senselessness to which they were subjected resists the capability of telling and the form in which telling occurs. In spite of the light they help shed on the horrific consequences of having been muted and thus being without a story, might one not say that the theories regarding the nature of stories and their telling are, at the same time, also ways to avoid these consequences themselves?

✦ ✦ ✦

Stories, then, would seem to be inadequate—if not morally inappropriate—forms in which to render the senseless brutality of the death camps. However, this insight is not meant to imply that one should simply have to give up the form of the story in order to articulate the monstrosity of the senselessness in question. In fact, this senselessness amounts to nothing less than an obligation on the part of the form of the story to seek to undo from within its sense-giving form. One example of such an effort to reshape the story's sense-creating form is Kertesz's shocking, because detached, prosaism in *Fatelessness*, which unsettles the reader's defensive preconception that the camps were hell itself in order to suggest something worse than hell. In this context one could, perhaps, also evoke the story that Zindel Grynszpan told during the Eichmann trial, a story no longer than ten minutes that, despite "creat[ing] nothing remotely resembling a 'dramatic moment'" nevertheless told of "the senseless, needless destruction of twenty-seven years [of a life in Germany] in less than twenty-four hours" very "clearly and firmly, without embroidery, using a minimum of words."[3] Of this story, which she transcribes in its entirety in her book on the Eichmann trial, Arendt notes that it showed "how difficult it was to tell the story [about the catastrophe] that—at least outside the transforming realm of poetry—needed a purity of soul that only the righteous possess. No one either before or after was to equal the shining honesty of Zindel Grynszpan."[4] Indeed, during the trial, he was, strictly speaking, the only one to tell his story. But telling stories of the catastrophe in the form of stories without inevitably making the catastrophe meaningful requires a transformation of the very form of the story. As Celan has shown, this can be achieved in what Arendt refers to as "the transforming realm of poetry." But what has been possible in poetry—namely, the ability to inscribe the senselessness of the holocaust and the muteness to which its victims were reduced—also needs to find its adequate formal means in the form of a story. In the genre of the story such a transformation might find, perhaps, an approximation in Kertesz's novel, paradoxically entitled *Liquidation*.

✦ ✦ ✦

The mutism of the returnees from the camps can be defined as an inability to confront their memories and as a defense against further pain, or further depletion of the self.[5] Such an explanation, however, does not fully grasp the incapacity in question and the fact that it is not an impairment that the subject has the power to simply change at will, or through clinical treatment for that matter. To mute a person is, as we have seen, to make him or her anonymous, ultimately, to eradicate his or her self, blotting out any possibility of having a story and of eventually telling it to others. A story would have been a form that would have made it possible for the survivors to make intelligible to themselves the monstrous cruelty and senselessness of what they underwent, thus resisting the dehumanization and depersonalization that struck them with muteness. The three theories about the story and storytelling leave no doubt that selfhood is not without a narrative. Without a story of one's own, or one told by others about oneself, no self can secure its identity even for a moment, let alone to secure the transmissibility of who one is to others, and for posterity. As a form independent of its specific content, a story is a structure that shapes a life into a repeatable intelligible unity and constitutes its meaning for oneself and others. It is an ideality that guarantees that a person's life gains distance from itself which, taking material shape in the form of a story, not only can be told, but once it is tellable, retold. A story always implies that it is about an other, or oneself as an other, and if narrated by oneself, the narrator is also different from oneself. In other words, the who one is, is in a way, the shadow of its story. Perhaps the most terrible specificity of Auschwitz, therefore, is that it was a systematic attempt to impair the formation of stories. The muteness of those who survived is testimony to this attempt to destroy what in the shadow of a story alone can coalesce into an identical who. Their untellable stories, therefore, demand unconditional respect.

✦ ✦ ✦

In spite of its horrific senselessness, Auschwitz confronts us with the obligation to seek to explain and comprehend it. In this case, such a task begins with the need to understand the difficulty of understanding what happened in Auschwitz. The task in question is, first of all, to "understand the frequent non-understanding" of what happened at that time.[6] But it should be kept in mind that any understanding of what led to Auschwitz and what took place there is not intended to reduce, or even eliminate its defiance of all intelligibility.[7] This also means that there is no story of Auschwitz if, as a story, it would contain a riddle that could be deciphered for an eventual message or moral for a specific addressee. Yet, if Auschwitz is of universal significance, it is not because it contains some lesson to be decoded by humanity as a whole, but because it has put humanity radically into question. What remains of Auschwitz is the universal shame regarding the fragility of meaning and the incapacity of sense to resist its own destruction.

✦ ✦ ✦

If stories have become an inadequate means of forming into a tellable unity what took place during the holocaust, it is because the senselessness of the event refuses all such form. The survivors' muteness is an index not only of the impairment of their faculty of telling, but of the untellable in the face of which the form of the story fails. No interdiction of storytelling is needed here. It itself acknowledges its inadequacy. No story measures up to an event, which by its senselessness defies all form with which to make sense of it and which, furthermore, would do injustice to the outrage the event inspires. And yet this event, which is of universal significance, needs to be told. But if it cannot be transmitted through stories, or at best, in transformed stories that are no longer stories in the usual sense, is there another discursive form in which this could be accomplished? Philosophy's constitutional exclusion of storytelling suggests that the other possible discourse in question would be the discourse of philosophy itself. However, this discourse is to remain pure of stories in order to communicate that which has to be said as it is in itself, or *as such*, for that which has to be said adequately. In our case this would be the infinite senselessness in the face of which storytelling became muted. But for philosophy to articulate something in its essence, or as such, it needs to expel from itself storytelling and its claim to speak the truth. But how is philosophy to accomplish this, if storytelling has already been impaired and resigned? The story's self-withdrawal in the face of the utter senselessness of the holocaust is thus, perhaps, the greatest challenge to philosophical thought! Through the failure of the story, philosophy is deprived of its defining exclusion of that, in distinction from which, it is *logos*, the saying of what something is in itself. Without the trace within philosophy of storytelling that has been expulsed from it, the philosophical logos loses its distinctive difference from the latter. With this, philosophy too would lose the possibility of speaking the truth about the senseless. If it were to try to do so, it would risk conferring an undesirable surplus of meaning to senselessness—in other words, philosophy itself would become a form of storytelling. But if philosophy's argumentative logic was to be replaced by narration, would that not mean the end of all stories as well?

✦ ✦ ✦

Called upon by his interrogators to tell "*just* exactly" what had happened, the narrator—a writer—of Maurice Blanchot's *The Madness of the Day* tells them the "whole story [*histoire*]." But having done so, the interrogators inform him that after this beginning he should finally "get down to the facts."[8] Forced to acknowledge that he lost "the sense of the story" as a result of what happened, the narrator is unable to form a tellable story on the basis of the events in question and concludes: "A story? No. No stories, never again."[9] The events he underwent are such that they irremediably affected the narrator's "sense of the story"—in other words, the faculty of sensing in the events the form of the story that would have allowed them to be shaped into a tellable tale. However loquacious, the narrator is thus muted. His "dumbness [*mutisme*]" is already manifest from the moment he begins to tell his interlocutors the whole story, since they tell him that he should finally tell the story of what happened to begin with.[10] What he tells them is not the story that they expect, or rather it is not a discourse that has the form of a story, and thus his telling is not a tale. In telling them the whole story, he, in fact, remains mute. But the story—the whole story—he tells his interrogators testifies that there will be no story anymore: in other words, no story that would uncover something. Indeed, "everything had long since been revealed," and what is uncovered, hence, for all to see, is not a story, and therefore also no longer tellable in the comfortable form of a story, or tale.[11]

NOTES

PRELIMINARIES

1. Plato, *The Collected Dialogues*, eds. E. Hamilton and H. Cairns (Princeton: Princeton UP, 1961) 986 (242c–d).

2. Plato 1033 (268d2–3). See also Stanley Rosen, *Plato's Statesman. The Web of Politics.* (South Bend, IN: St. Augustine, 2009) 57–58.

3. K. Ziegler and W. Sontheimer, eds. *Der kleine Pauly. Lexikon der Antike*, vol. 1 (Munich: Deutscher Taschenbuch Verlag, 1979) 177.

4. Henry George Liddel and Robert Scott, *A Greek-English Lexicon* (Oxford: Clarendon, 1968) 40.

5. Martin Heidegger, *Plato's Sophist*, trans. R. Rojcewicz and A. Schuwer (Bloomington: Indiana UP, 2003) 11.

6. Ruth Klüger, *Still Alive. A Holocaust Girlhood Remembered* (New York: Feminist Press, 2001) 64.

7. Ingeborg Bachmann, "Psalm" in *Darkness Spoken: The Collected Poems*, trans. P. Filkins (Brookline, MA: Zephyr, 2006) 55.

8. Bachmann.

9. Giorgio Agamben, *Remnants of Auschwitz. The Witness and the Archive*, trans. D. Heller-Roazen (New York: Zone, 1999) 17.

10. Primo Levi, "If This Is a Man," trans. S. Woolf, in Primo Levi, *The Complete Works*, vol. I (New York: Liveright, 2015) 25. Levi explains: "The explanation is repugnant but simple: in this place everything is prohibited, not for hidden reasons but because the camp has been created precisely for that purpose."

11. Hannah Arendt, *Nach Auschwitz. Essays & Kommentare I* (Berlin: Edition Tiamat, 1989) 7.

12. Hannah Arendt, *The Origins of Totalitarianism* (New York: Harcourt Brace Jovanovich, 1973) 444.

13. Arendt.

14. Arendt 445, 447, 457.

15. Dan Diner, *Gegenläufige Gedächtnisse. Über Geltung und Wirkung des Holocaust* (Göttingen: Vandenhoeck & Ruprecht, 2007) 28.

16. Léon Poliakov, "Humanity, Nationality, Bestiality" in *Questioning Judaism. Interviews by Elisabeth Weber*, trans. R. Bowlby (Stanford: Stanford UP, 2004) 97.

17. Christian Meier, *From Athens to Auschwitz. The Uses of History*, trans. D. Lucas Schneider (Cambridge, MA: Harvard UP, 2005) 137. Needless to say, the fact that the mass exterminations in the Nazi camps cannot be understood—that is, made meaningful—does not dispense one from the obligation to nonetheless try the impossible. Christian Meier observes that "as much as Auschwitz will always elude understanding, it is not acceptable to leave it at that" (160).

18. Arendt, *The Origins of Totalitarianism*, 457.

19. See Jean-Luc Nancy, *A Finite Thinking*, ed. S. Sparks (Stanford: Stanford UP, 2003) 16.

20. Soren Kierkegaard, *The Sickness unto Death. A Christian Psychological Exposition for Upbuilding and Awakening*, trans. H. V. Hong and E. H. Hong (Princeton: Princeton UP, 1980) 8, 27, 34.

21. Robert Antelme, *The Human Race*, trans. J. Haight and A. Mahler (Malboro, VT: Malboro, 1992) 289–90.

22. It is in this context that the demand arises for what María del Rosario Acosta calls a "new *grammar for listening*" […] "to what otherwise remains unheard in the testimonies of the survivors as well as in the reports of the secondary witnesses" (3, 11). See María del Rosario Acosta, "Arendt on Totalitarianism as

Structural Violence: Towards New Grammars of Listening" in A. O'Byrne and M. Shuster, *Logics of Genocide: The Structures of Violence and the Contemporary World* (Bloomington: Indiana UP, forthcoming).

23. See Georges Bataille, "Le sens de l'industralisation soviétique" *Critique* 4: 20 (Paris: Minuit, 1948) 72. (The essay also became part of *La part maudite*. See Georges Bataille, *Oeuvres Complètes*, vol.7 (Paris: Gallimard, 1976) 152).

24. Arendt, *The Origins of Totalitarianism*, 441.

25. Arendt. In her translation into German of *The Origins of Totalitarianism*, Arendt rephrases Bataille's statement as follows: "All explications of common sense, all comparisons based on history, all insistence of precedents serve finally only to 'superficially' refuse 'to dwell on the horrors.'" (Hannah Arendt, *Elemente und Ursprünge totaler Herrschaft* [Frankfurt/Main: Europäische Verlagsanstalt, 1955] 658.)

26. Arendt 441 (emphasis mine).

27. I note that a similar issue can be found in *The Sickness unto Death* where in an ethico-religious context, Kierkegaard speaks in the German translation of a human being "der mit dem ganzen Grauen einer erschreckten Einbildungskraft sich den einen oder anderen Schrecken als unbedingt nicht auszuhalten vorgestellt hat" (who "with the capacity to imagine terrifying nightmares has pictured to himself some horror or other that is absolutely unbearable"), and who is thus smitten by muteness (Soren Kierkegaard, *Die Krankheit zum Tode. Eine christliche psychologische Entwicklung zur Erbauung und Erweckung*, trans. L. Richter, *Werke IV* (Hamburg: Rowohlt Verlag, 1962) 37; Soren Kierkegaard, *The Sickness unto Death. A Christian Psychological Exposition for Upbuilding and Awakening*, trans. H. V. Hong and W. H. Hong (Princeton: Princeton UP, 1983) 38.

28. Let us also note that the expression, rather than referring to an *erschrockene*, speaks of an *erschreckte Einbildungskraft*. A merely frightened imagination is one that still remains intact as a faculty, but an *erschreckte Einbildungskraft* might suggest that what causes its fright has also shaken the power in question.

29. Chil Rajchman, *The Last Jew of Treblinka*, trans. S. Beinfeld (New York: Pegasus, 2011) v.

30. Hannah Arendt, *Essays in Understanding 1930–1954. Formation, Exile and Totalitarianism* (New York: Schocken, 1994) 14.

31. Imre Kertesz, *Eine Gedankenlänge Stille, während das Erschiessungskommando neu lädt. Essays* (Hamburg: Rowohlt, 2002) 44.

32. Klüger, *Still Alive*, 65. See also page 40 where she observes that one cannot come to grips with the Ghettos, the concentration camps, or extermination camps by way of any "traditional conciliatoriness and veneration of martyrdom."

33. Kertesz, *Eine Gedankenlänge Stille*, 90, 125.

34. This passage is missing from the English version of Krüger's book. It is to be found in the German original: Ruth Klüger, *Weiter Leben. Eine Jugend* (Munich: Deutscher Taschenbuch Verlag, 1992) 148.

35. Quoted after Agamben, *Remnants of Auschwitz*, 28. For a detailed philological discussion of the term "holocaust," as well as that of "Shoah," see Agamben, *Remnants of Auschwitz*, 27–36.

36. Understood as an *"event-without-a-witness,"* the term "Shoah" is reinterpreted by Shoshana Felman and Dori Laub on the basis of Claude Lanzmann's film. This term deserves perhaps a more open approach. (See Shoshana Felman and Dori Laub, *Testimony, Crises of Witnessing in Literature, Psychoanalysis, and History* [New York: Routledge, 1992] 224.)

37. Jean-Luc Nancy, "Un Soufle/Ein Hauch," trans. B. Stiegler, in *Shoah. Formen der Erinnerung: Geschichte, Philosophie, Literatur, Kunst*, ed. N. Berg, J. Jochimsen, B. Stiegler (Munich: Wilhelm Fink Verlag, 1996) 122–26; Walter Benjamin, "On Language as Such and on the Language of Man" in Walter Benjamin, *Selected Writings*, vol. I (1913–1926), ed. M. Bullock and M. W. Jennings (Cambridge, MA: Harvard UP, 1996) 73.

38. Walter Benjamin, "The Storyteller" in *Selected Writings*, vol. 3 (1935–1938) (Cambridge, MA: Harvard UP, 2003) 143–44.

39. Bemjamin 144.

40. The focus on the unique nature of what happened in the holocaust makes it possible to look differently at atrocities in other historical and geographical constellations. Rather than generalizing, hence equalizing all such catastrophes, the awareness of the holocaust's uniqueness permits us to look at them in an equally concrete fashion and to locate similarities between them that otherwise would not come to view.

41. Didier Fassin and Richard Rechtman, *The Empire of Trauma. An Inquiry into the Condition of Victimhood*, trans. R. Gomme, (Princeton: Princeton UP, 2009).

42. Fassin and Rechtman 19.

43. Denying the uniqueness of the holocaust (even though this uniqueness implies as such the possibility of repetition) risks being a form of subtle, and sometimes not so subtle, denial of its having taken place in all its historical concreteness.

44. Tadeusz Borowski, *This Way for the Gas, Ladies and Gentlemen*, trans. B. Wedder (New York: Penguin, 1976) 97.

45. For the methodical necessity of exaggeration in certain contexts and for certain issues, see Günther Anders. *Die Antiquierheit des Menschen. Über die Seele im Zeitalter der zweiten industriellen Revolution* (Munich: C.H. Beck, 1961) 15, 20.

46. Anders 124.

47. Levi, "If This Is a Man," 62.

48. Agamben, *Remnants of Auschwitz*, 52. In *Smothered Words*, Sarah Kofman has no place for the Muselmänner and, a fortiori, for the constant fear instilled in the other inmates of losing all their humanity. In her book, Kofman, who is concerned with arguing that in everything the inmates did and avoided doing in the camps, they resisted the SS effort to reduce them to mere larvae, is not only oblivious to the fact that no detainee could keep their humanity and dignity and avoid becoming morally corrupt if they were to have the slightest chance of survival, as well as the fact that in the case of the Muselmänner, the SS indeed succeeded

in making non-humans out of humans. (Sarah Kofman, *Smothered Words*, trans. M. Dobie [Evanston, IL: Northwestern UP, 1998].)

49. Robert Antelme, *The Human Race*, trans. J. Haight and A. Mahler (Marlboro, VT: Marlboro, 1992) 3.

50. Antelme 289.

51. Dorota Glowacka, *Disappearing Traces. Holocaust Testimonials, Ethic, and Aesthetics* (Seattle: U of Washington P, 2012) 102–33.

52. At the beginning of her fine study on trauma, narrative, and history, Cathy Caruth reminds us of the temporal characteristics of trauma not only according to Freud, about also its general definition: a trauma victim is haunted by the continual and uncontrollable return of the images of sudden violent events that happened to them in a recent past and that because of their incomprehensibility have to be reenacted by the sufferer because they have not been assimilated. The primary example for Freud of a trauma is thus an accident. Caruth writes: "The example of the train accident—the accident from which a person walks away apparently unharmed, only to suffer symptoms of the shock weeks later—most obviously illustrates, for Freud, the traumatizing shock of a commonly occurring violence" (*Unclaimed Experiences: Trauma, Narrative, and History* [Baltimore, MD: Johns Hopkins UP, 1996], 6).

But does this theory even come close to accounting for the holocaust victims' muteness? Harmed by what they experienced in the camps both physically and psychologically, they fall silent upon their return. Even though they obviously continue to be haunted by the incomprehensible events they underwent, they do not reenact them, but live with them. What distinguishes them from the sufferer of a sudden accident, the returning soldiers of World War I, and even the victims of post-traumatic stress disorder of recent wars, whose humanity has not been at stake in what was done to them, is the incomprehensibility of the condition to which they were reduced in the camps: to beings divested of all humanity! Their dehumanization exceeds anything of the order of a trauma.

53. As further proof of the returning soldiers' muteness, Benjamin points to the fact that "[w]hat poured out in the flood of books ten years later was anything but experience that can be shared orally." ("The Storyteller," 144). Something similar can perhaps be said of certain accounts by holocaust survivors.

54. Kertesz, *Eine Gedankenlänge Stille*, 62.

55. Imre Kertesz, *Fatelessness* (New York: Vintage International, 2004) 250, 256.

56. Agamben, *Remnants of Auschwitz*, 12.

57. Primo Levi, "The Drowned and the Saved," trans. M. F. Moore, in Primo Levi, *The Complete Works*, vol. 3 (New York: Liveright, 2015) 2420–21.

58. Kertesz, *Fatelessness*, 256.

59. The source of this statement, which Hannah Arendt uses as an exergue to the chapter on "Action" in *The Human Condition*, but also elsewhere, is unclear. It comes most likely from Daniel Gillès, who in "La Pharaonne de Rungstedlund," attributes it to Isak Dinesen. In his narrative of his visit to her at Rungstedlund, he reports: "Allais-je lui rappeler qu'elle avait écrit: 'Tous les chagrins peuvent être supportés, si on les met dans une histoire ou raconte une histoire à leur sujet?'" (See *Isak Dinesen, A Memorial*, ed. C. Svendsen [New York: Random House, 1965] 175–76.)

60. Odo Marquard, "Narrare necesse est" in *Philosophie des Stattdessen* (Stuttgart: Philipp Reclam jun., 2000) 61. See also Odo Marquard, "Die Philosophie der Geschichten und die Zukunft des Erzählens" in *Skepsis in der Moderne. Philosophische Studien* (Stuttgart: Philipp Reclam jun., 2007) 64.

61. Kertesz, *Eine Gedankenlänge Stille*, 55–56.

62. "The odium of incredibility," with which the news about the concentration camps was met, was part and parcel of the planning of the mass murder. Arendt remarks that "this doubt of people concerning themselves and the reality of their own experience only reveals what the Nazis have always known: that men determined to commit crimes will find it expedient to organize them on the vastest, most improbable scale." Arendt, *The Origins of Totalitarianism*, 439.

For the expression "odium of incredibility," see Arendt, *Elemente und Ursprünge totaler Herrschaft*, 646.

63. This process of degradation did not come to a stop with the living human being's total dehumanization; it continued in the way the corpses of the dead were treated: they were not to be referred to as corpses, but only as "Figuren," as figures, or dolls. (See Agamben, *Remnants of Auschwitz*, 51). Even the corpses were condemned to no longer belong to exemplars of a species called "human," let alone of the living in general.

64. Levi, "The Drowned and the Saved," 24–26.

65. Primo Levi, "The Truce," trans. A. Goldstein, in Primo Levi, *The Complete Works*, vol. 1 (New York: Liveright, 2015) 217. As Levi emphasizes, the "monstrosity" that the "offense" in question produced in the victim is something whose marks are indelible, and "would remain in us forever, and in the memories of those who were present, and in the places where it happened, and in the stories that we would make of it [...] It is foolish to think that it can be abolished by human justice. It is an inexhaustible source of evil" (216–17).

66. Arendt, *Nach Auschwitz*, 2–25. The silence of the survivors of the camps not only concerns what happened to them during the incarceration, but also often extends to their humiliation before and after the arrest. The systematic dehumanization of the victims of which Arendt speaks here makes it possible to understand their unwillingness or inability to even address their sufferings before the horror of the camps themselves. For a more extensive discussion of "the annihilation of the juridical person," "the murder of the moral person," and "the destruction of the individuality," or "of individual differentiation," see Arendt, *The Origins of Totalitarianism*, 447–55.

67. Arendt 24, 50.

68. Levi, "If This Is a Man," 23–24, 39. The numerous daily counts of the prisoners had no other reason than to force them into the realization that they were nothing but numbers.

69. Arendt, *Nach Auschwitz*, 50–51.

70. Levi, "The Drowned and the Saved," 2468, 2482.

71. Levi 2469.

72. Imre Kertesz, *Liquidation*, trans. T. Wilkinson (New York: Vintage International, 2005) 110.

73. Georg Wilhelm Friedrich Hegel, *Introduction to the Philosophy of History*, trans. L. Rauch, (Indianapolis, IN: Hackett, 1988) 64.

74. Hegel.

75. Even though I approach the question of stories through three distinctly different theories, it is obvious that Paul Ricoeur's work on narrative or, for that matter, that of Michel Henry, would have helped greatly to clarify the ontological status of stories in general.

76. Since these three thinker's concern with stories occurs almost simultaneously, it would be interesting to inquire into what lead to this conjecture, especially since all three are invested in, precisely, the phenomenon of stories and storytelling, rather than in narrative theory in general. Benjamin's essay appeared in 1936, Schapp's book on stories dates from 1953, and Arendt publishes *The Human Condition* in 1957. These works appeared over a span of approximately twenty years. All three of them highlight the vital role of stories in contrast to what has come to be known today as the great narratives or, in other words, history. Schapp developed his theory unawares of Benjamin's essay. Arendt, of course, knew Benjamin's essay, and by the time she translated *The Human Condition* into German—that is, in 1967—she might have familiarized herself with Schapp's work.

77. In order to determine Schapp's precise position within the movement of phenomenological thought and to evaluate the significance and the thrust of his contribution, I refer the reader to Hermann Lübbe, "Das Ende des phänomenologischen Platonismus. Eine kritische Betrachtung aus Anlass eines neuen Buches" in *Tijdschrift voor philosophie*, vol. 16, 1954, pages 639–66. Retracing

the history of the movement of phenomenology and, in particular, of Husserl's thought from static phenomenology to genetic phenomenology, a development in which Husserl is forced to recognize the importance of history, Lübbe shows how the aporias that classical phenomenology encounters in its search for the a priori eidetic structural constitution of the whole of the world, by taking its start in the intentional acts of consciousness, motivate Schapp to radically put an end to phenomenology as an inquiry into timeless idealities or essences. Schapp situates his research squarely in the phenomenon of history thus overcoming in the process phenomenology itself. But Lübbe discusses not only the philosophical implications of Schapp's contribution, but also its limits and the aporias it ushers in as a radical philosophy of history that absolutizes history.

CHAPTER 1

1. Translated by Jean Greisch, a French version of *In Geschichten verstrickt* appeared under the title *Empêtrés dans des histoires. L'être de l'homme et de la chose* (Paris: Editions du Cerf, 1992).

2. Lübbe, "Das Ende des phänomenologischen Platonismus," 650.

3. Jean Greisch, "Verstricktsein und Intrige. Ist eine reine Phänomenologie der Narrativität vorstellbar?" in Stefanie Haas, *Kein Selbst ohne Geschichten. Wilhelm Schapps Geschichtenphilosophie und Paul Ricoeurs Überlegungen zur narrativen Identität* (Hildesheim: Georg Olms Verlag, 2002) 118.

4. Thomas Rolf, "Wilhelm Schapps 'Beiträge zur Phänomenologie der Wahrnehmung'" in *Beiträge zur Phänomenologie der Wahrnehmung* (Frankfurt/Main: Klostermann, 2004) vii, x. For Schapp's critical relation to phenomenology, see Wilhelm Schapp, *In Geschichten verstrickt* (Frankfurt/Main: Klostermann, 2004) 169–73, 178.

5. What connects Schapp's work on law to his later writings is, as Michael Theunissen has argued, Schapp's concern in the context of his juridical writings with dialogism and language, a concern that despite being radicalized in his later writings to the point of transgressing the limits of his early phenomenological intentionalist approach, finds in the theory that the other is encountered only through his stories, a privileged expression. (Michael Theunissen, *Der Andere. Studien zur Sozialontologie der Gegenwart* [Berlin: de Gruyter, 1977] 401–06.

6. However, since the thrust of the analysis of the *Wozudinger* is to argue in a more general sense that all things appear only in the context of a story, the *Wozudinger* are not reducible to useful equipment.

7. Martin Heidegger, *Being and Time*, trans. Joan Stambaugh (Albany: SUNY Press, 2019) 5.

8. Paul Ricoeur, *Time and Narrative*, vol.1, trans. K. McLaughlin and D. Pellauer (Chicago: U of Chicago P, 1984) 74. For a discussion of both Schapp's and Ricoeur's theories of narrative, see Haas, *Kein Selbst ohne Geschichten*.

9. Wilhelm Schapp, *Philosophie der Geschichten* (Frankfurt/Main: Klostermann, 2015) 288–89

10. Schapp, *In Geschichten verstrickt*, 143 (emphasis mine).

11. Schapp 107–08.

12. For how the silent speech that accompanies not only all loud speech, but also all hearing, and that thus endows the latter with activity regarding the dialogical correspondence of a self to an other, see Theunissen, *Der Andere*, 404.

13. The term "Bestrickung" by contrast, apart from its colloquial meaning of knitting for a whole family, means above all to captivate by a charm, or more strongly, to bewitch. It is in this sense that Benjamin uses the term occasionally in reference to what the networks of myth do to those who are ensnarled in them, and from which only stories know the way out.

14. Schapp, *In Geschichten verstrickt*, 120–21.

15. Marquard, "Die Philosophie der Geschichten," 62–63.

16. Schapp, *In Geschichten verstrickt*, 100.

17. Schapp 101.

18. Schapp 103.

19. Schapp 105.

20. Schapp 146.

21. Schapp 148.

22. Schapp 126.

23. Schapp 125.

24. Schapp.

25. Schapp 126 (emphasis mine).

26. Schapp.

27. Schapp.

28. The concept of horizon is one of the very few phenomenological concepts that Schapp continues to borrow from phenomenology. "Abbau" is another such term, which *In Geschichten verstrickt* he repeatedly invokes.

29. Schapp 117.

30. Schapp 94.

31. Schapp 94.

32. Schapp 120.

33. Schapp 121.

34. Schapp.

35. Schapp 121, 123.

36. Schapp 123.

37. Wilhelm Schapp, *Philosophie der Geschichten* (Frankfurt/Main: Klostermann, 2015) 288–89

38. Schapp 31.

39. Levi, "If This Is a Man," 111. He adds that whereas, "[f]or living men the units of time always have value […] for us hours, days, months spilled

out sluggishly from the future into the past, always too slow, a worthless and superfluous material that we sought to rid ourselves as quickly as possible" (111).

40. Levi, *If This Is A Man*, 85.

41. Schapp, *Philosophie der Geschichten*, 39.

42. Schapp 293.

43. Schapp 26.

CHAPTER 2

1. However, whether Benjamin simply bemoans the loss of the vanished world of craftsmanship is questionable because of the history of the decline of storytelling that he sketches out in the essay. Artisenship has never been a foolproof guard against the powers that since immemorial times continue to threaten storytelling. But just as is the case with Heidegger, who considers thinking to be a craftsmanship and a lost art, a sense of loss and nostalgia nonetheless pervade his account of the end of storytelling.

2. Benjamin, "The Storyteller," 146 (trans. mod.).

3. Benjamin 147.

4. Benjamin.

5. Benjamin.

6. Benjamin 155.

7. Benjamin 143.

8. Benjamin 144.

9. Benjamin 145.

10. Benjamin.

11. Benjamin 147.

12. Benjamin.

13. Benjamin. In distinction from information which in order to be "understandable in itself"' is "shot through with explanation," storytelling must "keep a story free from explanation [*Erklärungen*] as one recounts it" (147–48). Benjamin thus links a hearer's relation to stories to what Dilthey, as opposed to explanation, terms "understanding" (*Verstehen*). After having pointed out that in Leskov's stories nothing is forced onto the reader, Benjamin remarks that "[i]t is left to him to interpret things the way he understands [*versteht*] them" (148). When events come to us shot through with information, there is nothing anymore to be understood about them. The perplexity, implausibility, or complexity of stories, by contrast, draws the attention of the listener, and trying to understand or interpret them, they are in a position to do something for him. Arousing astonishment on the basis of their implausibility, stories provoke reflection (*Nachdenken*) (148). The inherent implausibility of stories also makes for their "amplitude," their breath of oscillation or vibration (*Schwingungsbreite*): they have different messages for different hearers or readers (148). By not explaining themselves, stories, which Benjamin compares to seeds, preserve the power to germinate again and again.

14. Benjamin 145-46.

15. For Schapp, entanglement of stories is at best threatened by philosophy and the sciences' abstract relation to the real world.

16. Benjamin, "The Storyteller," 157.

17. Benjamin.

18. Benjamin 158.

19. Of Leskov, Benjamin observes that "[i]n keeping with Russian folk belief, he interpreted the Resurrection less as a transfiguration than as a disenchantment [*Entzauberung*], in a sense akin to that found in fairy tales" (158).

20. Benjamin 157.

21. Benjamin 157 (trans. mod.). Benjamin writes that "the fairy tale polarizes *Mut* (courage), dividing it dialectically into *Untermut*—that is, cunning—and *Übermut*." *Übermut*, in this context, is not to be rendered by "high spirits," as

the translator suggests, but as excessive courage. Like the Greek distinction between *metis* and *hubris*, both *Untermut* and *Übermut* are ways to deal with disproportionally overwhelming forces or powers. As my retranslation of both German terms into Greek suggests, Benjamin conceives of the ways in which the fairy tale provides counsel on how to escape the fetters of myth, which he interprets in terms of the Judeo-Christian conception of the fall of man, primarily, if not exclusively, from a Greek perspective. It is in an act of *hubris* that the tragic hero raises his head from out of the entanglement of mythic fate and through *metis* as a specifically Greek form of reason, he prevails in the face of paralyzing powers.

22. Benjamin.

23. Benjamin 161. "Chrysoberyl" is the translation for "Pyrop," which in the original is the name of the stone. The term "Pyrop" is significant here because this stone, also called "cat's eye," takes its name from the Greek "pyropos," eyes of fire, to which Benjamin alludes when he cites Leskov, who writes that "the alexandrite […] is known to sparkle red in artificial light" (161).

24. Benjamin 147.

25. Benjamin 149.

26. What Benjamin describes as the interconnectedness of guilt spun by the archaic forces is of the order of a tight web or texture. Yet the weaving of stories is, paradoxically, the principal way to counter these nets of the mythical in which humans find themselves entangled.

27. Benjamin 146.

28. Benjamin 150.

29. Benjamin 150.

30. Benjamin 149.

31. Benjamin.

32. Benjamin 150–51.

33. Benjamin 150.

34. Benjamin 151. The expression "dry dwellers" alludes to the practice in the late nineteenth century of letting people temporarily dwell for a reduced rent in built structures in which the walls had not yet had the time to dry. Their body heat helped accelerate the drying process of the still-wet plastered walls. Benjamin uses the simile to suggest that modern people dry up eternity from its relation to death, thus divesting themselves of their humanity in a way similar to the dry dwellers' sacrifice of their health.

35. Benjamin 151.

36. Benjamin 151.

37. As Hegel points out in the *Encyclopedia*, Mnemosyne produces signs through which a people can make their experiences narratable, a condition without which they cannot have a history. Signs, however, are not yet forms, even though through the signs of memory an experience acquires the form of a story. See *Hegel's Philosophy of Mind*, trans. W. Wallace and A. V. Miller (Oxford: Clarendon 2007) 2007.

38. With this notion of form, Benjamin's indebtedness to Georg Lukacs's *The Theory of the Novel*, and by way of it to Hegel, is plain.

39. Benjamin 151.

40. Benjamin 152.

41. Benjamin 153.

42. Benjamin.

43. Benjamin. Both approaches have in common that they make the course of the world intelligible through interpretation as opposed to the approach of the historiographer, who seeks to explain it. Furthermore, natural history is not simply opposed to eschatological history, but a secular variation of it. But as regards "the golden fabric of a religious view of the course of things," it too cannot easily be distinguished, at least in Leskov's stories, according to Benjamin, from "the multicolored fabric of a worldly view" (153). Natural history, after all, is the history of all *created* things.

44. In light of the paradigm that originates in Rainer Maria Rilke's *The Notebooks of Malte Laurids Brigge*, death in the camps is a denatured death. Rilke's *Notebooks* is certainly a source to which Benjamin's evaluation of death in modernity is indebted, except that the death in the camps cannot anymore be categorized by way of the term "death." See also Agamben, *Remnants of Auschwitz*, 72–73.

45. Benjamin cites approvingly Pascal's contention that "'[n]o one [...] does so poor that he does not leave something behind,' adding that "[s]urely it is the same with memories too—although these do not always find an heir" (154). With the decline of the art of storytelling, it is the role of the novel "to take charge of this bequest" (154). But as the profound melancholy that accompanies this attempt reveals, the characters featured in novels are those of persons who, in Benjamin's words citing Arnold Bennett, "had almost nothing in the way of real life" (155).

46. Benjamin, "On Language as Such," 72.

47. Benjamin.

48. Benjamin.

49. Benjamin 73 (trans. mod.).

50. Benjamin.

51. Benjamin.

52. Since muteness in Benjamin's essay concerns the telling of one's own story, the one who has been muted has not therefore necessarily lost speech altogether. He or she can still provide information of what he or she underwent, such as the images Borowski alludes to.

53. Levi, "If This Is a Man," 85. Let me recall again that most of the Muselmänner were Jews. Why they have been called by that name has been explained on the basis that their state of resignation resembled that of Muslims praying bereft in the face of the Almighty of all agency. But for an illuminating discussion of the theological and political history that made such an identification possible in the first place, see Gil Anidjar, *The Jew, The Arab. A History of the Enemy* (Stanford: Stanford UP, 2003) 138–62.

54. Antelme, *The Human Race*, 40. As Vasily Grossman remarks in his powerful essay, "[the] conveyer belt of Treblinka functioned in such a way that beasts were able methodically to deprive human beings of everything to which they have been entitled, since the beginning of time, by the holy law of life" (Vasily Semyonovich Grossman, "The Hell of Treblinka" in *The Road: Stories, Journalism, and Essays*, ed. R. Chandler (New York: New York Review of Books, 2010, 144). But if Grossman forgets to list death among the things or values, of which human beings sent to the death camps were deprived, it is because of his contention that the victims fought Fascism "by dying as human beings" (139). On the contrary, I hold that by being slaughtered, not even like cattle but in a way in which perverse and senseless cruelty became instrumentalized in the camps and served as a means to smoothen the industrial process of the extermination by crushing both the will and consciousness of the victims, the victims of the camps were deprived of a death that would have testified to their remaining humanity. Even though it is absolutely imperative to recall in full graphic detail all the humiliations and brutalities to which human beings were subjected in the camps by other human beings, the denial of death overshadows those horrors in that it is this denial that makes them, precisely, so horrendous and so senseless. A similar point needs to be made with respect to Antelme's claim throughout *The Human Race* that the victims of the camps remained beings of the species of humans, and that the SS remained powerless to rob them of their belonging to that race (See Antelme, *The Human Race*, especially pages 218–19).

CHAPTER 3

1. For the distinction between political and nonpolitical action, see also Hannah Arendt, *The Human Condition* (Chicago: U of Chicago P, 1958) 188.

2. Hannah Arendt, *Vita Activa oder Vom tätigen Leben* (Munich: Piper, 2007) 224.

3. Arendt, *The Human Condition*, 182–83.

4. Arendt, *Vita Activa*, 225.

5. In chapter 26 of *The Human Condition*, titled "The Frailty of Human Affairs," Arendt emphasizes that the beginner who starts an action also calls on others for help in carrying out his or her initiatives. Action, therefore, has, as she does explicitly state in *Vita Activa*, a "double-faced character" (235). This double-faced character of action further emphasizes not only that it takes place within a preexisting web, but that it has itself also the character of a weave.

6. Arendt, *The Human Condition*, 176.

7. Arendt.

8. Arendt 179.

9. Arendt writes in *The Human Condition*:

> Speechless action would no longer be action because there would no longer be an actor, and the actor, the doer of deeds, is possible only if he is at the same time the speaker of words. The action he begins is humanly disclosed by the word, and though his deed can be perceived in its brute physical appearance without verbal accompaniment, it becomes relevant only through the spoken word in which he identifies himself as the actor, announcing what he does, has done, and intends to do. No other human performance requires speech to the same extent as action. (178–79)

10. Arendt, *The Human Condition*, 179–80.

11. E. R. Dodds, *The Greeks and the Irrational* (Berkeley: U of California P, 1951) 42, 40.

12. Arendt, *Vita Activa*, 219.

13. Arendt, *The Human Condition*, 180.

14. Arendt, *Vita Activa*, 220.

15. Arendt, *The Human Condition*, 180–81; Arendt, *Vita Activa*, 222.

16. Arendt, *Vita Activa*, 223.

17. Arendt.

18. Arendt, *The Human Condition*, 182.

19. Arendt; Arendt, *Vita Activa*, 224.

20. Arendt, *The Human Condition*, 182.

21. Aristotle, "De Interpretatione" in *The Complete Works*, vol. 1, ed. J. Barnes (Princeton: Princeton UP, 1984) 26 (17a4).

22. See Rodolphe Gasché, *Persuasion, Reflection, Judgment. Ancillae Vitae* (Bloomington: Indiana UP, 2017) 9–63.

23. It follows from this distinction between two kinds of *logoi* that in the same way that the practical *logos* in the sphere of the political is not, as Arendt does not tire of arguing, dominated by the values of truth and falsehood, stories and storytelling too not only do not consist of propositions capable of truth, but they are entirely foreign to such an epistemic concern.

24. Arendt, *The Human Condition*, 183–84.

25. Arendt, *Vita Activa*, 226.

26. At this point it also becomes clear that the web of human relations should not be qualified as "social." The social, as Arendt understands it, is an extension of the interrelations constitutive of the private sphere to that of the whole of the human fabric. By contrast, the web woven from the new beginnings that human beings make by appearing in the world of others, and the relations to others that they instate through their speeches, is of a public and political nature.

27. Arendt, *The Human condition*, 188.

28. Action understood as a kind of weaving reminds one, of course, of the problematic of *symploke* in Plato's *Statesman*, except that for Plato only a good statesman masters the art of weaving. As opposed to the plural humans who

for Arendt in being with one another are all involved, by weaving through their actions and speeches, in the web of human interrelations, a web that is not a whole and does not know hierarchies, the statesman, in her interpretation, as a strong man, who dominates the realm of human affairs, is as its head isolated from it. Furthermore, his task is to shape it into a harmonious whole. Here weaving is an artisanal function, as a result of which the interrelated whole of human affairs takes on at the hands of the statesman the form of a work. (Arendt, *The Human Condition*, 221–30)

29. Arendt, *The Human Condition*, 184.

30. Arendt.

31. Arendt, *Vita Activa*, 226–27.

32. Arendt, *The Human Condition*, 184.

33. This distinction between the living reality of stories and stories as artifacts or things among other things is crucial for Arendt's elaborations on the subject, but it must also be pointed out that she does not always consistently pursue this eminently phenomenological distinction. This is especially the case when the issue is to explain how a lived story, once it is completed by the death of its subject, congeals into an object like others.

34. Could these acts by which an agent unknowingly reveals him or herself to others, and the act of others by which they shape a story that the agent cannot but suffer, be characterized as dissymmetric? In which case a fundamental distance and tension between different activities and their planes would animate the life of the political.

35. Arendt, *The Human Condition*, 186.

36. Arendt 184.

37. Arendt 190.

38. Arendt 191.

39. Arendt, *Vita Activa*, 239.

40. Arendt, *The Human Condition*, 191–92.

41. Arendt, *Vita Activa*, 239. Even though Schapp's work, *In Geschichten verstrickt*, appeared five years before the publication of *The Human Condition*, Arendt did not seem to have known it at that moment. Yet in the additions (like the ones quoted) that she made to her translation of her work into German published in 1967, in which there are several references to being "entangled in stories," seems to indicate that in the meantime she had become familiar with Schapp's book. One may, of course, speculate on the reasons why she does not give credit to Schapp for the expression. Perhaps one reason is the entirely apolitical conception of the human being in Schapp's work.

42. Arendt, *Vita Activa*, 239–40.

43. At this point the distinction between Benjamin's and Arendt's conception of the story becomes tangible. It is certainly striking that Arendt does not even once refer to Benjamin's "The Storyteller." Among the distinctions between the two is the fact that stories for Benjamin are characterized by implausibility, rather than suspense as is the case in Arendt. Suspense for Benjamin is a feature of the novel! Furthermore, for Benjamin stories do not have an end. They contain counsel of how to continue a story. Only the novel has an end—Finis!

44. Arendt, *The Human Condition*, 192.

45. Arendt, *Vita Activa*, 240–41.

46. Arendt, *The Human Condition*, 192.

47. Arendt 193.

48. Arendt.

49. Arendt; Arendt, *Vita Activa*, 242.

50. Arendt, *The Human Condition*, 193.

51. Arendt, *Vita Activa*, 241.

52. Arendt, *The Human Condition*, 193.

53. Arendt, *Vita Activa*, 242.

54. Hannah Arendt, *The Promise of Politics* (New York: Schocken, 2005) 172.

55. Arendt, *The Human Condition*, 193–94.

56. Arendt 194.

57. Arendt 194. Let me point here at another difference between Benjamin's and Arendt's elaborations on the story: the Benjaminean storyteller weaves a thread of his or her own experiences into the story he or she crafts, and on which he or she leaves, like the potter on the pot, his or her own fingerprints.

58. Arendt, *Vita Activa*, 243.

59. Arendt.

60. Adriana Cavarero holds that it is quite astonishing, if not troublesome, that given her emphasis on natality, Arendt would uncritically subscribe to the Greek heroes' "love of death" in order for them "to earn an imperishable memory" (Adriana Cavarero, *Relating Narrative. Storytelling and Selfhood*, trans. P. A. Kottman [London: Routledge, 2000] 28–29). In fact, as should be clear from what has been developed so far about Arendt's understanding of how stories are engendered, the heroes' concern with death is a perversion, as it were, of the realm of the political and of the constitutive role that others have in the weaving of another's story. In this context, let me also point out that Cavarero fully agrees with Arendt that self-identity is a function of a story that is properly one's own but that needs an other to be told. Put differently, only biography can provide such a story, as a result of which Arendt, as Cavarero notes, has no place for autobiography in her account of the significance of the story for self-identity. Yet by conceiving of the self as an intrinsically "narratable self" in *Relating Narratives*, Cavarero defines the self as intrinsically constituted by the desire for a story. She writes that "narratable identity is linked to an explicit desire for narration from another's mouth" (137). Undoubtedly, the autobiographical impulse, which drives a self to narrate its story to itself in a desire for unity, is a narcissistic fallacy. But as Cavarero shows, in the relations between the self and an other, particularly in intimate relations such as friendship and love, the other becomes a narrator and biographer who tells the self his or her life story, and thus provides the self

with a story that it can subsequently tell to itself (and others) as its autobiography. However, if Arendt gives short shrift to autobiography, it is not because she would disagree with Cavarero's more complex and dynamical description of interrelational storytelling, but precisely because in the context of her account of the Greek hero's deceptive fabrication of his own story by way of a freezing look at his daimon, the autobiographical impulse and its fallacy are necessarily construed in parallel to the former's limitation of the role that others play in the formation of his story.

61. Arendt, *The Human Condition*, 194. As Arendt makes amply clear, Plato's and Aristotle's reflections on politics are also based on the model of craftsmanship. See, in particular, Arendt, *The Human Condition*, 195.

62. Is not much of what has been reported about those who perished in the camps of the order of what Benjamin calls "information"?

63. For Arendt's use of the term of "spontaneity," see for example, Arendt, *The Origins of Totalitarianism*, 455.

POSTLIMINARIES

1. Jacques Derrida, *Dissemination*, trans. B. Johnson (Chicago: U of Chicago P, 1981) 241.

2. Kertesz, *Liquidation*, 26.

3. Hannah Arendt, *Eichmann in Jerusalem. A Report on the Banality of Evil* (New York: Viking, 1971) 228–30.

4. Arendt. For a discussion of Arendt's remarks on Grynszpan's story in the context of the dialogical in-between space, which the authors consider to be the condition of possibility for the emergence of stories (in distinction from testimonies), see Bonnie Honig and Ariella Azoulay, "Between Nuremberg and Jerusalem: Hannah Arendt's Tikkun Olam," *differences* 27:1 (2016) 66–67.

5. See, for example, Bruno Bettelheim, *The Empty Fortress. Infantile Autism and the Birth of the Self* (New York: Free Press, 1967) 59.

6. Meier, *From Athens to Auschwitz*, 160–61 (trans. mod.).

7. Or should one not rather proceed on the assumption that it can be made intelligible, but not therefore meaningful?

8. Maurice Blanchot, *The Madness of the Day*, trans. L. Davis (Barrytown, NY: Station Hill, 1981) 18.

9. Blanchot.

10. Blanchot 17.

11. Blanchot.

INDEX

Achilles, 101–105
Acosta, Maria del Rosario, 124n22
Aesop, 3
Agamben, Giorgio, 20, 32
Alexander II, 67
Ananke, 47
Anders, Günther, 127n45
Antelme, Robert, 13, 29–30, 80, 140n54
Archilochus, 3
Arendt, Hannah, 7, 9, 15–16, 18, 34–35, 38, 41, 48, 75, 81–109, 114–117, 125n25, 129n59, 129n62, 130n66, 131n76, 141n5, 142n23, 142n26, 142n28, 143n33, 144n41, 144n43, 145n57, 145n60, 146n61, 146n63, 146n4
Aristotle, 17, 100, 146n61

Bachmann, Ingeborg, 5
Bataille, Georges, 15, 125n25
Bennett, Arnold, 77, 139n45
Benjamin, Walter, 20–23, 31, 38, 41, 48, 55, 57–81, 93, 103, 106, 114, 116, 129n53, 131n76, 133n13, 135n1, 136n13, 136n19, 136n21, 137n23, 137n26, 138n34, 138n43–45, 139n52, 144n43, 145n57, 146n62
Blanchot, Maurice, 120
Borowski, Tadeusz, 27–28, 139n52

Caruth, Cathy, 128n128
Cavarero, Adriana, 60
Celan, Paul, 111, 117

Derrida, Jacques, 111
Dilthey, Wilhelm, 41
Diner, Dan, 7
Dinesen, Isak, 32–33, 81, 129n59

Eichmann, Adolf, 117
Eumaeus, 3

Fassin, Didier, 24–25
Felman, Shoshana, 126n36
Frege, Gottlob, 13
Freud, Sigmund, 21, 25, 128n52

Gaus, Günter, 18

Gillès, Daniel, 129n59
Grossman, Vasily, 140n54
Grynszpan, Zindel, 117, 146n4

Hebel, Johann Peter, 74
Hector, 192
Hegel, Georg Wilhelm Friedrich, 37, 138n38
Heidegger, Martin, 2, 4, 43–45, 98, 135n1
Henry, Michel, 131n75
Himmler, Heinrich, 7
Hitler, Adolf, 8
Homer, 3, 102
Husserl, Edmund, 2, 41, 43, 45, 56, 131n77

Kant, Immanuel, 17
Kertesz, Imre, 18, 31–32, 34, 36, 111, 114, 117
Kierkegaard, Sören, 12, 125n27
Klüger, Ruth, 5, 18–19, 126n32, 126n34
Kofman, Sarah, 127n48

Lanzmann, Claude, 126n34
Laub, Dori, 126n36
Leskov, Nikolai, 66–68, 74, 136n13, 136n19, 137n23, 138n43
Levi, Primo, 7, 20, 28–29, 31–32, 34–35, 52, 80, 114, 123n10, 130n65
Lukacs, Georg, 59, 77, 138n38

Lübbe, Hermann, 42, 131n77

Marquard, Odo, 33, 47
Meier, Christian, 8, 124n17

Nancy, Jean-Luc, 11, 20

Odysseus, 3
Origines, 66

Parmenides, 1
Pascal, Blaise, 139n45
Patroclus, 102
Plato, 1–3, 43, 142n28, 144n41, 146n61

Rajchmann, Chil, 17
Rechtman, Richard, 24–25
Rickert, Heinrich, 41
Ricoeur, Paul, 44, 131n75, 133n8
Rilke, Rainer Maria, 139n44

Schapp, Wilhelm, 38, 41–56, 63, 93, 106, 114, 116, 131n76–77, 132n4–5, 133n8, 134n28, 136n15, 144n41
Scheherazade, 28
Simmel, Georg, 41

Theunissen, Michael, 133n5

Valéry, Paul, 70–71

Wiesel, Elie, 20, 111

www.ingramcontent.com/pod-product-compliance
Lightning Source LLC
Chambersburg PA
CBHW051102230426
43667CB00013B/2405